LOVING LIFE

LOVING LIFE

TALES OF MY WONDROUS JOURNEY

Gay Hendricks

Waterside Productions

First Printing, 2025

ISBN-13: 978-1-968401-08-5 print edition
ISBN-13: 978-1-968401-09-2 ebook edition

Waterside Productions
2055 Oxford Ave
Cardiff, CA 92007

TABLE OF CONTENTS

PREFACE

Welcome to *Loving Life*, memories and stories of adventures I've had in my eight decades on earth.

I've enjoyed a life of magnificent depth and richness, and I'm grateful beyond words for every moment of it. From my other books, such as *Conscious Loving, The Big Leap* and *Five Wishes,* you already know lots of details about my adventures in relationship, especially the tales of how Kathlyn (also known as Katie) and I created the juicy life we've enjoyed together since 1980. There are some relationship stories in the book, but the main focus is on the singular side of my life, the feasts of sound, sight, touch, and taste I've reveled in, the unusual places and spaces, inside and out, that I've been privileged to visit.

As I write this, I just turned 79, a good long life by any standards. However, a long life is probably overrated unless you also add depth and richness to it. I've known people who lived a long life but whose moment-by-moment experience was drenched in bitterness and despair. Creating a life that's rich and full and joyful is where the big satisfaction is. It's also where the Big Fun is.

Big Fun is one of my highest values; I define it as having a great time while simultaneously creating a space for others to have a great time. In that spirit, I've had Big Fun in writing every word of this memoir, even the parts that brought forth tears as I typed.

A note on the title: I was trying out titles on my friend of thirty years, the master tunesmith and lyricist, Kenny Loggins.

"I'm thinking of calling it *Savoring Life*. What do you think?"

Kenny closed his eyes and meditated on it for a moment. Then he opened his eyes and said, *"Savoring Life* is good, but why not call it *Loving Life?* That's really what you've been doing all these years."

I took his inspired suggestion and *Loving Life* it is. A deep bow to Kenny for the title and many other inspirations over the years.

And now to the stories. I hope you enjoy reading them as much as I enjoyed living them.

PART ONE

CHAPTER ONE

MY SECRET BIRTHDAY WISH

When I was a little boy, I always made the same wish when it would come time to blow out the candles on the birthday cake. Where I grew up, the custom was to close your eyes, make a secret wish in your mind, then try to blow out all the candles with a big "whoooosh." If you blew out all the candles, your wish would come true. That was the procedure, and I took it very seriously.

Here's what I did, every year on my birthday. I'd close my eyes and make the following wish in my mind:

"Eternal happiness for everybody, including me."

Then, I'd blow like mad to get those candles out. I didn't usually have any trouble extinguishing all the candles (except for one time when my brother installed fake ones that wouldn't blow out.)

You were also supposed to keep your wish secret afterwards, and I scrupulously observed this rule for many years. Finally, Dewey, one of my neighborhood buddies, pressed me hard to reveal my wish. Since I'd kept it secret so many other times, I didn't figure it would hurt to let it out just once. I told Dewey I wished for all of us to be happy all the time.

He was flabbergasted. "I know you want a BB gun and a bike," he said. "Why didn't you wish for one of those? You shouldn't waste your wish on something like happiness. And besides, nobody can be happy <u>all</u> the time."

The budding psychologist in me had already thought this through.

I explained that I always wished for happiness because if I was happy then it wouldn't matter if I got a bike or not. I also explained my theory about being happy all the time: If you'd ever felt happiness, even for a second or two, it meant that you could feel happy all the time. It was just a matter of tweaking the machinery.

Dewey's response was "You're out of your mind." I couldn't argue with that, but unlike him, I didn't think it was necessarily such a bad thing. If he and other people were securely <u>IN</u> their minds—and they weren't happy and didn't think it was possible to be happy—maybe being a little out of your mind could be useful.

The "Dewey" barrier is probably the first one you're likely to run into if you decide you want to be happy all the time. You're likely to hit that barrier if you launch any other bold program of self-change. The very day my friend, Richard, made a commitment to sobriety at his first AA meeting, two of his alcoholic friends tried to talk him out of going to the meeting. Fortunately, he didn't let them. Fourteen years later now, he's still sober and going to meetings.

Expect that any time you make a bold commitment, someone will step up and tell you it just isn't possible. The person who tells you this will likely not be a happy person, so if you can muster the courage, I suggest that you not take the advice. Taking advice on happiness from a person who's not happy is like getting advice on vegetarianism from a guy who's chomping on a pork chop.

The same is true for relationships. Like my lofty goal for being happy all the time, I wanted to create a relationship with a woman where the flow of loving connection was always there. I ran up against the "Dewey" problem there, too. Just about every person I described my goal to told me it was unrealistic. It took a lot of work (and a partner, Katie) who was as committed as I was, and eventually we created a relationship that ran on continuous positive energy. From 1980 onward we focused on that goal, but the dedication paid off beyond my wildest dreams. We haven't had an argument or exchanged a cross word this century.

There are some of you who are just out of your minds enough to commit to being happy all the time. You're also committed to creating relationships in which your genius and the genius of your partner is allowed to flourish continuously. You don't care whether other people think it's possible. <u>YOU</u> think it's possible and you're passionate about finding out if you can pull it off.

You're my people.

Here's another vivid childhood memory:

I'm about seven years old, still young enough to hold my mother's hand. We're walking along a street in the sleepy Southern town where I grew up. Mom is a much-loved newspaper columnist who will later become mayor; it's impossible to walk more than half a block with her without getting stopped by someone who wants to talk to her about politics. Mr. McGill stops to talk to her; he's an elderly realtor whom I had seen around town but never officially met. After introductions, he stoops down to ask me the big question.

"And you, young fellow, what do you want to be when you grow up?"

Without a moment's hesitation I reply, "An expert!"

Mr. McGill and my mother burst into laughter, but I don't get it. I'm not joking.

"An expert in what?" he asks, a grin crinkling his face.

"It doesn't matter," I say, triggering another gale of laughter.

After we departed from Mr. McGill, Mom asked me how I'd developed this lofty career goal.

"The man in the tie," I said.

"Explain," she said.

I got interested in being an "expert" during a visit to my mother's newspaper office. School was nearby, and I'd often stop by afterwards to see if she was finished for the day. One afternoon I was sitting near her desk, waiting for her to finish typing, when I noticed a man in a tie moving briskly about the office. Nobody ever wore ties in my mother's office; I could hardly keep my eyes off his tie and his crisp, white shirt. The newspaper office wasn't air-conditioned, and in the steamy heat of Central Florida, 'crisp' and 'shirt' are two concepts that usually do not occur together.

There was something about his manner, too. Even his step looked purposeful, in contrast to the ambling gait favored by my local townspeople. I asked my mother who he was and what he was up to. She said he was an "efficiency expert" from the home office, here to help the newspaper work better.

I remember watching him carefully as he went about his work. He would stop at one person's desk, engage in a brief conversation, then move on to talk to another person. After he moved on, the person's energy would seem to pick up, as if the expert had transmitted something that immediately affected his or her behavior. I think it was the first time I realized that ideas and words, if they were focused and clearly expressed, could immediately change someone's behavior. To my young mind, that seemed like a game worth playing.

When I got to be a teenager I forgot, at least on the conscious level, about my quest to understand happiness. I fell into the usual teenage concerns about cars and pimples and whether girls liked me. It took me well into my twenties to wake back up to the life purpose I'd set in motion when I was a kid. Once I got refocused on understanding how to be happy, though, I haven't thought about much else for the past fifty years.

So, there are two things I feel qualified to speak about as an expert:

- How to be happy
- How to enjoy lasting love with a mate

These are two of the most important things in life, yet for some reason we get almost no formal education in them. I had to accumulate my expertise in the rough-and-tumble school of life. By my mid-thirties I had learned enough about happiness that I was able to get happy and then get back to being happy after the inevitable upsets. I had also learned enough about love to attract a fabulous woman and stay deeply in love with her for the past forty-plus years. Even though I've done lots of things that others might consider important, the two things of most value to me are the flow of happy feelings inside me and the flow of loving connection with the people close to me.

I don't know if my birthday wish—for all of us to be happy all the time—will ever come true. I don't have any control over what seven billion other people do with their hearts and minds. However, I think it's such a good idea that it can't help but catch on someday. In the meantime, it has to start somewhere, and I decided to let that somewhere be me. I put my attention on growing my ability to keep a flow of good feeling going inside me, with a particular focus on finding out what I did to interfere with that flow. I also mounted a search for all the ways I sabotaged the flow of loving feeling between me and my beloveds. My quest paid off abundantly. It took a few years to clear up the debris left by a lifetime of happiness-preventing habits such as overeating, lack of exercise and relationship drama. It took a few more years to acquire the healthy habits I rely on to this day, including two half-hour periods of meditation and an hour of exercise every day, as well as eating nutritious food instead of a diet based on burgers, fries, and ice cream.

It took me until the age of thirty-four before I cracked the relationship code. In my teens and 20s, my relationships tended to resemble the trajectory of the Titanic. They always started with great fanfare but kept hitting the same iceberg over and over. Slowly it began to dawn on me that the iceberg was me. Looking back, I can hardly believe it took me so long to figure out such a simple observation. However, as the wise Sally Kempton writes, "It's hard to fight an enemy with outposts in your own head." After relationship dramas with a dozen women over a fifteen-year period, I finally woke up and put my attention on what I did to sabotage the flow of love. There, I struck gold.

I realized I sabotaged the flow mainly by concealing and lying about important things, most often my feelings. I bottled up my anger, my hurts, and my fears, stonewalling the repeated attempts by friends and lovers to ask me how I felt inside. I also realized that all this concealed feeling inside me affected how I saw the person across from me in the relationship. Because I was stonewalling my own internal feelings, I often projected onto the woman I was with that she was concealing things from me.

A friend of mine, after listening to me talk about a few relationship disasters, said, "I know what one of your problems is. You have a bad picker." It was funny, but it was also dead-on true. Unconsciously, I picked women who, like my mother, were burdened by addictions. My unconscious pattern was to get attracted to women with addictions of various sorts—alcohol, Valium, cigarettes—and then expend large amounts of energy blaming them for the addiction and trying to get them to stop.

All that changed a month before I turned thirty-five. I've written about this moment in detail in other books, but in brief, I made a new commitment that changed my life. I vowed to be absolutely honest in my relationships, to take responsibility for things that came up instead of blaming and projecting, and to find a woman who was as passionately committed to her own creative life as I was to mine.

A month after I made that commitment, I walked into a crowded room and saw a woman with a special glow about her. She looked radiantly healthy and had a smile that lit up her face. I made a point of meeting her. Based on my new commitment to transparent honesty, I blurted out the first honest thing I could think of.

I said, "I'm really attracted to you."

Katie said, "Oh!"

I proceeded boldly ahead. "I'd love to ask you out for coffee, but first I need to tell you something. I just figured out how I mess up relationships, by not telling the truth, by blaming the other person when stuff comes up, and by burning up a lot of my creative energy in relationship dramas. I just made a commitment to creating relationships based on telling the truth, taking responsibility for the stuff that comes up, and being passionately devoted to my creativity. On those terms, would you like to have coffee with me?"

There was a long pause while Katie tried to decide whether the person in front of her was, in her words, "totally crazy or very, very sane." Apparently, she came down on the side of sane. She said, "How about lunch?"

Lunch went extremely well, and our subsequent adventures in intimacy are described in *Conscious Loving*, *The Conscious Heart*, and our book about relationships at mid-life and beyond, *Conscious Loving Ever After*. We celebrated our 40th wedding anniversary in 2021 and are excited to see what the future will bring.

The skills that allowed our love to thrive became the foundation of our relationship work with couples, families, and ultimately in the world of business. We spent the 1980s testing out our ideas and techniques until we had accumulated practical experience with about a thousand people. One evening, sitting in front of the fireplace after working with ten couples, Katie and I hatched an idea that would have profound consequences for us. We decided to write a book about the seven main principles we had developed and the tools we used in our sessions. We envisioned a new kind of book, written so that it gave a new toolkit to our fellow professionals *and* the general public simultaneously.

At the time, there was a large gulf between academic books and self-help books. In front of the fire that night, we dreamed up a book we felt would bridge that gulf—a book that would be equally useful to other professionals and to our clients. We spent the year of 1988 writing the book, and from the beginning it had magic associated with it. Our agent, Sandy Dijkstra, held an auction and sold it to a publisher for more money than we'd ever seen at one time in our lives. The magic continued when we had the good fortune to have the legendary Toni Burbank as our editor. We admired the work she'd done on the books of two friends of ours, John Bradshaw and Deepak Chopra, and in her hands she transformed the book and took it to a new level. Toni and our agent, Sandy Dijkstra, even came up with a perfect title for the book.

When we turned in the manuscript, our title was *Enlightening Relationships*. It was clunky and a mouthful of syllables, so I appealed to Sandy and Toni to invent a better title. They came through magnificently; I can still remember the excitement in Sandy's voice when she called to ask me what I thought of their new title, *Conscious Loving*. Katie and I both loved it.

More magic happened when the book was ready for publication. Our publicist, Leslie Rossman, booked us on 'Oprah' with her first phone call. A short time later we were on our way to Chicago. Up until we walked on Oprah's stage for the first time, my idea of a bestseller was *Learning To Love Yourself*, which sold ten thousand copies a month. After 'Oprah' aired, the publisher told us they were taking 10,000 orders an hour! Thirty years later, *Conscious Loving* is still in print and selling steadily, thanks to Sandy, Toni, and Oprah, three amazing women who changed our lives.

Although the second part of this book will delve more deeply into our work, what follows is a succinct list of the key principles and practices that *Conscious Loving* brought to the world. These are now widely taught in graduate programs, as well as being used by singles and couples around the world. One of our most treasured possessions is the collection of emails and letters from couples who have used our processes to change their lives. We've even heard from a few hundred couples who have used the principles and techniques as the basis of their wedding vows!

The First Principle

Relationships thrive when each partner commits to total union with the other person and total creative expression as an individual.

The First Practice

Make a heartfelt commitment to your partner that you're willing to go beyond all your ego-defenses to full unity. At the same time, make a commitment to go all the way with your own individual creative expression. Then observe the emergence of your defensive barriers every day. Communicate about them honestly, but don't take them seriously. In fact, ego-defenses disappear quickly when you turn them into play.

The Second Principle

Relationships thrive when each partner learns from every relationship interaction, especially the stressful ones, instead of running programmed defensive moves. Some popular defensive moves: criticizing, lying, sulking in silence, making noisy uproars, numbing out with food, drink, smoke, TV, and other habit-forming drugs.

The Second Practice

Make a heartfelt commitment to learning something new from every relationship interaction. Notice your defensive moves as they emerge, and gradually transplant wondering and truth-speaking in place of defensiveness.

The Third Principle

Relationships thrive in a climate of absolute honesty – no hidden feelings or withheld truths. All feelings – anger, sadness, joy, fear, sexual attraction – are okay to discuss with the other person, and each person is able to listen, free of listening-filters such as listening-to-find-fault and listening-to-fix.

The Third Practice

Notice your feelings and thoughts, and then speak about them to your partner. If there are things you've done or feelings you're afraid to talk about, make <u>sure</u> to speak about those to your partner. Get familiar with your habitual listening-filters, and practice summarizing what the other person is saying, with no distortion, and acknowledging the feelings embedded in communication.

The Fourth Principle

Relationships thrive when people keep their agreements impeccably. It doesn't matter whether an agreement seems trivial ("Sorry, honey, but I forgot to take the trash out.") or significant ("Sorry, honey, but I slept with your twin sister and the maid of honor the night before our wedding.") There is no such thing as a minor lapse of integrity.

The Fourth Practice

Monitor each agreement you make very carefully, making sure you want to make it in the first place. Once you make an agreement, fulfill it impeccably or change it consciously by communicating with the relevant person.

The Fifth Principle

People thrive in a climate of 100% accountability, where nobody blames or claims victim status. 100% accountability is the shift from "I was wronged" to "I take full responsibility for events occurring the way they did." From this empowered position, problems can be solved quickly, because time and energy are not squandered in a fruitless attempt to find fault.

The Fifth Practice

In any situation, claim responsibility for having created it the way it occurred. Wonder about how and why you might have wanted it to occur that way. Speak in empowered language rather than victim language ("I choose to go to the dentist" rather than "I have to go to the dentist." "I take responsibility for eating so that I have a healthy body," rather than "Why did you buy that huge bucket of buttered popcorn? You know I can't resist it.")

The Sixth Principle

Relationships flourish when partners appreciate each other liberally. People grow more beautiful through our appreciation of them. Relationships take a quantum leap when each partner practices appreciation of the other person as a daily art form.

The Sixth Practice

Invent new ways to appreciate the other person every day and speak appreciations frequently. Live inside questions such as, "What is my partner's true essence and how can I invite it forth?" And "What could I appreciate about my partner at this moment?"

The Seventh Principle

Everything can be resolved with willingness and love. Love is the ultimate healer and liberator because only love is vast enough to embrace its opposite. In other words, you can love yourself even when you hate yourself, and the hate will melt in the larger presence of love. Whatever emerges in a close relationship is the next thing that needs to be loved.

The Seventh Practice

Love as much as you can from wherever you find yourself.

Katie and I live by those principles and use the practices every day. We've found them incredibly helpful, not just in romantic relationships but in all relationships. For example, we and our colleagues at the Conscious Leadership Group have taken these ideas and practices into more than a thousand businesses and non-profit organizations. As we like to say, "The same principles and tools work in the bedroom, the boardroom, and the kitchen."

CHAPTER TWO

FAMILY MATTERS: MEMORIES OF A "VERY UNUSUAL GROUP OF PEOPLE"

When I was eleven and in the sixth grade, a distant cousin named John visited us at the family compound in Central Florida. He was in his twenties, from my grandfather's side of the family in Missouri, and none of us had ever met him. My mother hosted a gathering in the backyard, attended by my grandparents, my aunts Audrey and Lyndelle, their husbands, and my aunt Kat, about whom you'll learn much more shortly. The only person missing was my brother, Mike, who was away at college.

The day is vivid in my memory, partly because our cousin came to the gathering in his Navy uniform. It was 1956, the height of the Cold War with Russia, and here was a frontline fighter standing in my own backyard! Later, I would find out that Cousin John was a clerk in the motor pool, but at the time I could hardly take my eyes off his spotless white uniform.

I also remember something he said to me in parting.

After two hours of conversation and the full onslaught of Southern picnic favorites—deviled eggs, baked ham, barbecued chicken, peas, corn on the cob, pecan pie, and gallons of sweet iced tea—Cousin John had to leave to return to his naval base in Pensacola. I accompanied him down the front lawn to his car and we said our goodbyes. He got behind the wheel, but before he drove off, he leaned out the window and said one last thing. He shook his head in wonderment and said, "That's a very unusual group of people you've got there."

I knew exactly what he meant.

There was my grandmother, Dell, whose eccentricities were legendary. For example, she backed into another car in 1925 trying to get out of a tight parking place. Thereafter and for the rest of her life, she refused to use the reverse gear. If she got into a situation that required backing up, she called a family member to come downtown and do it for her. After I got my driver's license, I inherited the job.

My grandmother had lived in Leesburg almost since its founding and had a sense of ownership of her community I've never seen since. I remember a trip downtown with her when I was in elementary school. She couldn't find a place to park on Main Street, but she spotted a policeman on the corner and waved him over. She turned off the engine, got out of the car in the middle of Main Street and handed him the keys. "Park it for me, please."

Without a blink of hesitation, the cop said, "Yes, ma'am," got in and drove off to find a parking place.

When we got through shopping, the cop was standing outside the store to escort us to the car.

Dell's husband, my grandfather, Elmer Canaday, was also at the party, a silent presence who spoke perhaps a hundred words a year to all family members combined. I'll have more to say later about my grandparents and their influence on me, but for now, let me just give you a window-peek into their relationship.

In 1937 my grandparents got a new Chevrolet. My grandfather had stopped driving, due to weak eyes, so my grandmother had to ferry him everywhere. The new Chevy was her pride and joy, the result of a long battle with my grandfather, who considered Henry Ford a god-like figure. Sometime during the first week, though, an event occurred that put a permanent blemish on the Chevy. The event was still resonating in their relationship in 1950, when it came to light due to a curious 5-year-old's question.

I often rode in the back seat when my grandmother was driving my grandfather to work. One day I asked about a brown streak on the passenger's side window. It had been there as long as I could remember, but I'd never heard where it came from and how come it wouldn't wash off. I knew it wouldn't come off because I'd helped my granddad wash the car several times.

The moment I asked about it I saw my grandparents stiffen. My grandfather muttered something like "It was a long time ago," and I quickly changed the subject. Later, though, I wangled the story out of my grandmother, and it was a therapist's dream. To understand the drama, we have to begin with what I call the Tobacco Wars. Throughout my childhood my grandparents fought about my grandfather's habits of chewing tobacco and smoking cigars. He had a wad of Star chewing-tobacco in his jaw all day long, as well as puffing on a Hav-A-Tampa cigar every hour or so. My grandmother loathed tobacco in all its forms. To her it was more than foul smoke or brown spittle; it was an emblem of the class difference between her and my grandfather. She came from the plantation-owning class of Southern royalty; he grew up on a Missouri dirt farm. (The South ultimately won the Tobacco Wars. When I was in elementary school my grandfather was banished from the house and forced to carry out his vices on the back steps.)

The first week they had the new Chevy in 1937, Granddad was riding in the passenger seat and spat a stream of tobacco juice out the window. His eyesight was not good, however, and he failed to notice that the pristine new window was actually rolled up. The tobacco juice hit the window with a splat and slid down slowly out of sight. A furious argument ensued.

On the surface it seems like a problem that could be easily solved with a quick apology and ten seconds of dedicated scrubbing. Not in my grandparents' world! These two stubborn and consummately cantankerous people got into a conflict about who should clean up the streak. Dell's position was that Elmer should clean it up. In her view (which frankly seemed very reasonable to me), he had made the mess so it was his job to clean it up! Elmer had a very different position, which turned out to be incendiary: cleaning windows is "women's work," and HE DIDN'T DO WOMEN'S WORK! Neither would budge, and the streak was still there when my grandmother got a new car twenty-five years later.

My aunt Audrey was at the party; she was my grandparents' eldest daughter and a star of the family. Audrey spent most of the year in Washington, running the office of the congressman who represented the area. Her husband, Bob, a man of fewer words than Granddad, would be there hovering in the background.

Aunt Lyndelle was there, her natural vivaciousness kept aloft by a steady, secret intake of vodka. Her husband, Hal, would be standing nearby, puffing on one Chesterfield after another. Hal was a man of such profound taciturnity that he made Bob and Granddad look like chatterboxes.

My mother, Norma, played host that day. She was the other family star, a journalist who wrote a daily column for the local paper and was just a year away from becoming mayor of the town. Audrey, Lyndelle, and Mom were all heavy smokers, but were not allowed to smoke around my grandmother. At any gathering longer than a half hour or so, they would begin to twitch and grimace as the grip of their addiction tightened, slipping away one at a time, ostensibly to use the bathroom in my mother's house, but actually sneaking a cigarette.

The only other family member at the picnic was Aunt Kat.

Although she was thirty years older than I, Kat was my best friend and playmate when I was a little boy. Kat had Downs Syndrome, born at a time when such children were called "Mongoloid." She was my grandparents' fourth daughter, born when my grandparents were nearing forty, and became an issue between them. I don't think they ever got beyond it. I know it was still causing conflict when I arrived on the scene thirty years later.

My grandmother was the most loving person you could imagine—toward her children and grandchildren. She loved Kat just as unconditionally as she loved her three brilliant older daughters. She also loved me and my brother extravagantly. However, her unconditional loving did not extend to my grandfather, her sons-in-law or practically anyone else, especially those of the male gender. When my aunts' husbands, Hal and Bob, were forced to appear for Thanksgiving or Christmas dinners, my grandmother never addressed them by name. Instead, she would say, "Audrey, see if Bob might want some more string beans." Thus, she could obey the dictates of Southern hospitality while not actually acknowledging their existence.

My grandmother was capable of hair-trigger Old Testament wrath. I could spot the early warning signs of it, so I made sure I stayed clear when she went off. One thing that would evoke her rage was any suggestion that Kat wasn't perfect exactly as she was. I remember the time some older kids were walking up our street and taunted Kat as they passed. They yelled something like "Hey, retard!" and got a big laugh. My grandmother, who was probably 70 years old at the time, came off the front porch like a raging bear and gave the teenagers a verbal lambasting that had them sprinting out of range at full gallop.

By contrast, I never heard my grandfather utter a kind word to Kat. My grandmother told me that he had been so outraged at having a "Mongoloid" baby that he had shunned her from birth. Kat was a living reminder of imperfection to a man who demanded perfection from everybody around him. My grandmother became Kat's lifelong protector, and when I came along, I adopted that role, too. Some of my most painful memories from childhood come from moments when I tried to shield Kat from my grandfather's rage. Fortunately, Kat had the all-encompassing love of my grandmother; she and Kat never spent a day apart until my grandmother's death in 1966. When my grandmother died, it was if Kat unplugged from the source. She died shortly after my grandmother's passing.

I loved Kat dearly. She was an eternal child, a fun-loving sister, a constant ray of sunshine in a gloomy environment. There were no kids my age in the neighborhood until I was in elementary school, so Kat and I were boon companions and inventors of endless games together. When I went off to school, though, everything changed. Suddenly I was playing with other kids my age, and without realizing it at the time, I left Kat behind. I registered it unconsciously, though—I can still recall a vivid picture of a sad-faced Kat, sitting on the front porch with my grandmother's arm around her as I trooped off to school with my Roy Rogers lunchbox.

My grandfather was a genuine curmudgeon. He'd grown up on an impoverished Missouri farm and had run away at sixteen to avoid being a farmer. He said he noticed early on that farmers either died young from accidents or tended to live long lives, filled with never-ending labors. Neither alternative looked attractive to him, so one day he took temporary ownership of one of the farm's mules and lit out for "any place that wasn't Missouri."

He joined the army and headed south to take a troop ship to the Philippines, where the Spanish-American War was heating up. Along the way he made a fateful stop in Springville, Alabama. There, he met Rebecca Dell Garrett, a Southern Belle from a family that had been wealthy plantation-owners before the Civil War. Dell described herself as "the only remaining unmarried woman in the county." She confessed to him that she was notoriously cantankerous and hard to please, but instead of turning him off it had the opposite effect. My grandfather was without question the most cantankerous, hard-to-please person I've ever known, so I'm not surprised he was attracted to my grandmother. Elmer and Dell had a three-day courtship and promised to write each other until he returned. He then left for war.

I often tried to extract war stories from my grandfather— "Did you ever shoot anybody, Granddaddy?" He always stonewalled me or said something bland like "Believe it or not, the Philippines are even hotter than Florida." In general, he had a dim view of the whole enterprise of war. According to him, the main benefit of war was to rid the world of excess teenage boys.

Elmer made good on his promise and returned to marry Dell, who had managed to hang onto her position as the last unmarried woman in the county. They set off in a horse-drawn buggy for Florida, where my grandfather had lined up a job managing an orange grove. They went on to be married more than sixty years, (although my mother always joked that they spent fifty-nine of those years not speaking to each other.)

I loved both my grandparents unreservedly, in spite of their eccentricities. Up until I went to elementary school, I spent most of my time at their house, even though my mother's house was only a hundred feet away. In old-fashioned Southern style, all members of my family—my mother, my aunts and their husbands lived in houses within shouting distance of the Big House where my grandparents lived.

I often got caught in the crossfire between my grandparents. On the positive side, though, my early efforts to resolve squabbles between them prepared me well for a career in the helping professions. Like many families, mine ran on secrets and roundabout communication. Nobody ever said anything important directly to the relevant person. For example, one of my aunts quietly drank herself to death without anyone discussing it openly, even though she lived within a stone's throw of everyone else. I cannot count the number of conversations I had as a kid that ended with the caveat, "But don't say anything to _____ about this."

One of the through-lines that ran through the family was the need to please my grandmother. She was the magnet around which all the iron filings of the family oriented themselves. Although she was incredibly loving, everybody but Kat and me was also scared of her. Kat and I had a special relationship with her: we could do no wrong. Nobody else fit that category. I was bonded to my grandmother much more than I was to my mother. If I'd had my preference, I would have stayed at my grandparents' house all the time. Up until I was in second grade, I probably spent five nights out of seven with my grandparents. My grandmother's health began to decline, though, so I reluctantly went to live at my mother's house full-time.

Pleasing my grandmother was essential, but I also wanted to please my grandfather. He was the only male role model around, the gruff but tolerant old guy who gave me my first baseball glove and played endless games of catch with me. By the time I came along he'd become the manager of the town's baseball park, the home of a minor league team. I spent my days at the ballpark all summer long, helping Granddad with everything from groundskeeping to making change at the gate.

One season when I was still a pre-teen, I even got to sit up in the press box and run the scoreboard ball-and-strike lights. I got paid the awesome sum of fifty cents a game for my services. Since games usually lasted three hours, I was very likely the lowest paid person in Leesburg, Florida. I didn't mind, though, because I was already well into a lifelong love of baseball. Being involved with the game in any way was thrill enough.

As I grew into my teens, I mostly saw Kat when I would stop off at the Big House after school. We'd sit with my grandmother in a swing on what was called the Screen Porch. It was a veranda the length of the front of the house, screened in against the slavering hordes of mosquitoes outside. I usually stayed for an hour or so before going off to my other pursuits.

One memory from that era that can still evoke a wave of grief in me: the day I left for college. I was packing the car when my mother said, "Go see Kat. She doesn't understand." I walked over to the Big House, where Kat and Granny were next to each other on the swing and saw the same sad face I'd seen when I walked off to go to first grade. Kat looked stricken, snuggled up against my grandmother's shoulder. It broke my heart, but handling emotions was not my high-skill area at the time; I was probably in the least emotionally intelligent phase of my life. All I could think to do was hug her and tell her I would be back, that I was only going forty miles away and would love her wherever I was. I can still feel that pain sixty years later; my heart aches when I think of the dreadful unfairness of life that causes one person to be favored and one not.

I have a happy memory I draw on, from the final years of Kat's life. Her favorite show on television was Romper Room, a children's program hosted by Miss Nancy. Children who visited the show got a "Do-Bee" pin, encouraging them to be a positive, polite person who accomplished useful things—an emblem of the high value of the show. Kat wanted a Do-Bee pin more than anything in the world, but given her age and situation, there was no possibility of her getting one. Then came a benign strike of fortune.

I went to Rollins College in Winter Park, near Orlando where Romper Room was produced. One day I started a new class and found myself seated beside Miss Nancy, who was taking the class during a hiatus from the show! I told her about my aunt and her passionate fandom; the next week Miss Nancy came to class with a Do-Bee pin for Kat. I feel tears spring to me eyes just now as I'm writing, remembering the look of wide-eyed delight on Kat's face when I gave her the pin.

One of my treasured possessions is a photo of Kat holding me when I was a baby. She has a huge smile on her face. Everybody else in the picture looks glum, but there is Kat, beaming like she's getting to hold the Baby Jesus himself. I still feel the power of her love today; it helped shape me into who I am. Kat's love is in every breath I take.

CHAPTER THREE

HOW TO BE HAPPY EVEN WHEN YOU HAVE THE FLU

Once upon a time, Katie and I went to New Zealand, supposedly on a vacation. Thanks to frequent-flyer miles, we'd earned a couple of free first-class tickets to anywhere in the world. First, we thought about going to Bora Bora, because a friend had spoken of it in glowing terms. Then, another friend raved about a recent trip to New Zealand, and we decided to go there instead. I'm not into having regrets, but if I were, I'd put that decision right up at the top of the list.

The journey seemed cursed from the moment we stepped onto the airplane in San Francisco. After we boarded and got ready to take off, the crew discovered a mechanical problem that caused us to taxi back to the gate. They got it fixed, taking an hour or so to make the repairs. Back out on the runway, we'd missed our slot and faced a delay while twenty-three airplanes (yes, I was counting) took off ahead of us. From the time we got on the plane until our wheels left the ground it was just under three hours. Then, it took something like twenty-two hours of air travel to get to New Zealand, including a stopover in Honolulu.

There must have been flu bugs rampant on the airplane, because by the time we stumbled off the plane in Auckland we were sneezing, hacking, and clutching tissues to our streaming noses. The last couple of hours of the flight, the first-class cabin sounded more like a dog kennel than the oasis of serenity we'd hoped for. Our flight even made the news, because a couple hundred of our fellow passengers also came down with the new strain of bug called the Shanghai flu.

We dragged ourselves to the hotel and spent the next three days pretty much flat on our backs. We saw on TV that the new bug was sweeping the country. It sure swept us. All my joints ached so badly that even the slightest movement made me groan. Also, even the most ordinary sounds—cars outside the window, a vacuum cleaner in the hall—sounded like somebody was banging trash can lids. At one point I had to put the clock in the bathroom because every tick sounded like fingernails on a chalkboard. Neither one of us spoke much because the act of forming words was painful.

To make matters worse, we had planned our first three days in the spa town of Rotorua, a resort famous for its hot springs. People came from all over to bask in the hot water and healing mud. However, we had somehow overlooked that these were hot *sulfur* springs. As you probably know, hot sulfur smells like rotten eggs. When the wind was in a certain direction, gusts of sulfurous air would sweep through our hotel room, even if the windows were tightly closed. Since the flu had turned the volume on my senses up to the max, it felt like the entire universe was one giant rotten egg.

Hours passed, then a day. Reading made my eyes ache. Food was out of the question and television was dreary. Accordingly, I had a great deal of time to think. It didn't seem to hurt me to think, so I began occupying my mind with how I could be happy in a situation like I was in. After a while I had a big insight. If I opened my awareness to all the unpleasant sensations I was feeling, I ceased judging them as "unpleasant."

The achy feeling in my joints just became a batch of sensation, neither bad nor good. As long as I kept my awareness wide open, I transcended feeling awful and slipped into a state of simply *feeling*.

Hours began to pass like a flowing river, not in one excruciating tick at a time. At one point the phrase "I'm happy" popped out of my mouth. Katie, lying beside me, said "Me, too." She'd come to the same realization, that if she kept her awareness wide open she didn't feel bad. Over the next couple of days practically the only words that came out of our mouths were "I'm happy" and "I love you." Those were the only two things we could say that didn't hurt.

After three days we were back on our feet again and went on to explore the wonders of New Zealand, a land that famously has "more sheep than people" and from my personal experience, more flies than sheep. After we recovered, we trekked around both islands by bike and car, discovering many delights such as Milford Sound, one of the most beautiful places on earth.

In spite of our good time afterward, the flu left such an impression on us that we've never had the urge to return. In the years since our visit, we've been invited to return many times to give seminars, speeches, and such. When I get one of those invitations, I close my eyes and call to mind the sounds and smells of that long-ago vacation. Then I open my eyes and compose a note of polite regret.

CHAPTER FOUR

THE TINY TITAN OF CRACKLE: A NIGHT AT THE OPERA

I'd like to tell you about the most wonderful night of operatic music I've ever experienced. Although it happened many years ago, hardly a week goes by without my remembering it and savoring the enjoyment of it. And getting a good chuckle, for reasons that will soon be clear.

I don't remember ever listening consciously to a piece of classical music until I was in my teens. There certainly wasn't any to be heard in my house, and even if there had been a record or two, they would have been played on a little phonograph with tinny speakers. All that changed when I was fifteen, though, when the London Philharmonic played a concert in Daytona Beach, near where I grew up. My mother scored tickets through her connections as a newspaper columnist and took a friend of mine and me with her to the concert.

It was transformative.

To go from zero experience of classical music to hearing the London Philharmonic was like stepping out of the desert into a magic garden. It opened up a whole new world of sensory richness for me. I remember marveling all night long at the artistry of the individual musicians and the dedication it must have taken to become that good. I came away with a few notes of despair resonating inside me, too. I played baritone horn in my high school marching band. I was a pretty decent horn-blower, but I could hear immediately the vast gulf between me and the musicians on stage. I had entertained some thoughts of a career in music, perhaps in a band or as a producer, but hearing the London Philharmonic put a stop to that fantasy. I decided to focus instead on being an appreciative listener. It was probably a wise decision, because if you think you have a choice between music and some other career, you're probably not a real musician.

Now, to opera. As you probably know, opera is an acquired taste, such as caviar or cognac. I'm wild about caviar, while my wife is equally vocal in her distaste for it. (That worked in my favor in the golden days of yore when airlines served caviar in first class; I always got two helpings!) Opera is the caviar of sound. People who don't like it are very sure they don't like it, but the people who like it usually REALLY like it.

The first great opera I saw in person was *Samson and Delilah* by Saint-Saens, performed at the State Opera of Vienna. It was a major treat for several reasons. First, European audiences listen to music with a degree of rapt attention I've never heard anywhere else. Entire concerts can go by without a single cough. Second, the performance itself was magnificent and flawless. The third reason I enjoyed the performance so much speaks to the way opera is viewed in Vienna and Europe in general. It's considered a cultural institution for everybody, not just for the social elite. To that end, they sell very inexpensive 'standing-room' tickets at the back of the house, equipped with cushioned benches where you can kneel if you get tired. I was a *pfennig*-pinching backpack traveler when I first came through Vienna, so standing-room was all I could afford. Being able to see one of the great opera companies of the world for a couple of dollars was a most welcome gift to a poor traveler. The big moment in the opera is Salome's *Dance of the Seven Veils*, the closest thing to a strip show in the opera canon. Although it was a tame strip by today's standards, it still raised the temperature in the hall by a good ten degrees.

Now, fast-forward a decade to the greatest night of opera in my life. Although I'd been in and out of New York dozens of times, I'd never managed to be there at a time when I could get to the Metropolitan Opera—until one magic night. Katie and I made a quick stop in New York on publishing business, a trip that was hurriedly arranged with no time to book advance tickets for any shows or concerts. At our hotel, I scanned through the newspaper to see if there was anything we might attend. I had my eye out for bargain tickets, because we had two kids in college at the same time and there wasn't much money left over for parental entertainment. In previous visits, I'd sometimes found a 2-for-1 deal on tickets or a half-price we're-about-to-close-the-play special. My heart leapt when I saw that *La Bohème*, one of my absolute favorites, was being performed at the Met. I called and found that the concert was sold out. However, the kindly ticket-person told me there was a last-minute line one could stand in. If a season-ticket holder did not show up, one had a chance of buying the ticket for a discounted price.

Katie and I grabbed a cab and sped up to Lincoln Center. We found the line and waited in it for about 45 minutes. People around us in line, all old hands, told us that they sometimes got tickets for as little as $10 or $15. Suddenly we found ourselves surging forward to the window. The ticket-person said, "We have two seats left, but they're in one of the most expensive boxes." "How much?" I squeaked.

"They're $350 seats but they're discounted to $55 each." It felt like a stretch, but who could turn down a $350 box at the Met? Minutes later we were seated in a box barely twenty feet from the stage.

The box held six chairs, two rows of three chairs each. None of the chairs was occupied when we were ushered into the box. The chairs did not appear to be numbered, so we took the two chairs on the left in the front row. As time for the curtain grew near, we began to wonder if we would have the whole box to ourselves. When the opera began, we were still all alone in the box.

I was awestruck pretty much from the moment the music began. The sets were spectacular in their beauty and complexity. The music was sublime. The soprano singing the role of Mimi had a beautiful voice and was a crowd-pleaser, too. There is no audience more flamboyant in their appreciation than an opera crowd; "Bravos" rang out through the evening. Everything was perfect, except for ....

The sound of the woman behind me rummaging in her purse!

I was so enthralled by the sights and sounds of the opera that I barely noticed when two people came in late, toward the end of Act One, and took their seats behind us. I glanced around to nod a "hello" and saw that the new arrivals were an elderly woman and a middle-aged woman, perhaps her daughter. As the first act proceeded to its thrilling conclusion, I got distracted repeatedly by the elderly woman behind me digging for something in her purse, almost making a comically loud racket as she did so. I glanced around at her several times, and each time was greeted with an odd expression from both women, kind of a sweet glare. I grew up the South, where the art of the Sweet Glare was perfected. I knew something was wrong, but I didn't know what.

The end of the first act is one of the most sublime moments in all opera. Mimi and Rodolfo, having just fallen madly in love, go off-stage singing a glorious duet that soars to a final high note of harmony charged with hope and longing. The last notes of the duet hang in the air as the lovers go toward their destiny.

I was keenly anticipating the moment, so as it approached, I gave my sonic torturer a sharp glance of disapproval. It did nothing to quiet the rummaging. Finally, she found what she was looking for and the sound abated. Flooded with sweet relief, I went back to my immersion in the opera. It lasted about ten seconds, because ....

Rip-rip-rip—she began trying to get the cellophane off a box of mints! On and on went the crackling of cellophane as she grappled with the complexity of the task. It ceased for a moment, and I whipped my head around to find out if my long ordeal was over. But no, she was rummaging in her purse for a nail file, entering the tool-using phase of human evolution. Opening her mints with this implement consumed another noisy minute or two. Finally, the wrapper was defeated, and the box was opened. Then the chomping of Junior Mints began, replete with loud, wet sounds of pleasure. This was no mere enjoyment of mints. It was a celebration of lip-smacking satisfaction raised to operatic heights.

As the first act approached its climax, I felt a nearly unbearable tension building in my body. Every cell in my body was yearning in anticipation of this transcendental moment, yet at the same time I could feel those same cells screeching with irritation at the amazing volume of noise this tiny woman behind me was putting out. Apparently, though, she loved the end of Act One as much as I did, because all noise from behind ceased as Mimi and Rodolfo began their magnificent duet. I surrendered to the music and let ecstasy overtake me.

As the curtain came down for the intermission, I stood up, partly to stretch my legs but mainly to check out the tiny lady who had so irritated me. She was barely five feet tall, impeccably dressed and looked to be 75-80 years old. When Katie and I introduced ourselves, they both bared their teeth in the kind of hostile smile I'd seen earlier. Clearly, I was missing some major cue. I left the box to get water, and during the intermission I went to find an usher. Were we perhaps in the wrong box?

The usher glanced at my ticket and at the door of the box. He pointed at the number on the ticket, showing me that it was the same as the box door had on it. "You're in the right place," he said.

He opened the door and peered inside, then glanced down at the ticket again. He whispered to me, gesturing with his chin toward the elderly woman and her daughter, "They're sitting in your seats. Would you like me to ask them to move?"

I felt a flood of embarrassment and relief wash over me. Now I understood. They weren't sitting in our seats—we were sitting in theirs! Her relentless onslaught of crackling, rummaging, and munching had been a "polite" way of expressing her irritation at us for hogging her spot! I felt my own surge of anger. It wouldn't have been that hard for her to lean over and whisper "You're in our seats. Let's swap." It illustrated my long-held conviction that there is a ten-second solution underneath almost all human problems.

"Where does it say which ones are our seats?" I asked.

He pointed to letters on the ticket, D and E. "That's D and E they're sitting in. The letters are on the chairs, kind of hard to see. She probably didn't notice in the dark."

No, we were the guilty party. "Thanks," I said, "I'll take it from here."

Telling the microscopic truth saved the day. I went back into the box and adopted my tried-and-true persona for such situations, Mr. Humble and Confused. I said, "My wife and are from out of town and haven't been to the Met before. We didn't see the little letters on the seats. I wonder if you could change places with us."

Suddenly they beamed happily, with none of the flavor of hostility that had confused me earlier. They introduced them-selves, mother and daughter as we'd suspected. First, they tried to tell us they didn't mind sitting in the back row, but I knew better than to fall for that one. Both Katie and I are descended from many generations of long-suffering martyrs who exact their revenge in covert ways. Plus, I had first-hand experience of just how much distraction this tiny individual could generate. I said, "Since there's nobody else in the box, let me arrange the chairs so we can all be on the front row." I did, and we all settled in to await the dazzling beginning of Act Two, a Parisian street-scene involving jugglers, clowns, and other colorful passers-by.

Both mother and daughter turned out to be charming companions, once we'd made the transition from squatters on their real estate to fellow opera fans. The rest of the eve-ning went by in a whirl of magical sound and magnificent sights, completely free from sound effects by the Tiny Titan of Crackle seated next to me.

CHAPTER FIVE

QUESTS FOR THE ULTIMATE

Katie and I have traveled a great deal together over the past forty-plus years. Early on, we both put a priority on developing professional work that didn't feel like work. We reasoned that if we loved our work, we'd always feel like we were on vacation. Ultimately, we brought our vision into reality, and even though we've taken very few trips that were purely "vacation," and even though we probably do something that involves our work 365 days a year, we feel like the luckiest people on earth.

On many of our trips we've given a humorous purpose to the excursion. For example, we turned a trip through the English Lake District into a quest for the ultimate piece of toffee. This purpose forced us to compare many different toffees from many different little shops. The purpose also caused alarm when we got home and weighed ourselves, but that's not a very interesting story.

One year, a bicycle ride through Scotland became a quest for the ultimate shortbread cookie. Since we were riding bikes all day, we didn't have to wear the cookies home in the form of excess baggage around our middles.

Thirty years ago in the Cayman Islands, we discovered a little bakery that made the most incredibly wonderful macaroons we'd ever tasted. They were not too sweet, as I find most macaroons. They were the perfect combination of crunchy on the outside and chewy on the inside. That experience compelled us to buy many macaroons in many different countries, so we could find out if there was a macaroon anywhere in the world that matched up. So far, I haven't found a better one, even on the streets of Paris, so I implore any of you who are Cayman-bound to make sure you visit the bakery on the main street of George Town. By now there's probably more than one bakery on the main street, so visiting all of them in search of the perfect macaroon could give a much-needed purpose to your vacation. They also had an excellent, moist banana bread on offer, one of my top five favorite baked items along with macaroons, pineapple upside-down cake, apple *tartin*, and my grandmother's Jefferson Davis pie.

Regarding the latter, I recommend that my readers immediately do an internet search for a Jefferson Davis pie recipe and give it a go. It's a simple recipe that's hard to screw up. One bite will change your life, and if there's any left to serve others, it will give you an exalted place in their hearts. It may also establish a presence in their arteries, too, given the insane amount of butter in a Jeff Davis pie, but I've eaten many of them and am still here in my 70s.

There's one experience we had in our travels, though, that ended a particular search on the spot. It occurred in northern Italy, in the charming town of Alba, during a bicycle tour. In the 80s, we took on the heroic task of writing three bicycle tour books of several European countries: Italy, France, and the British Isles. Our agent sold the books to a New York publisher on the strength of a proposal and got us a $25,000 advance to help cover the costs of the tours. It didn't, of course, but it was a useful fantasy to get us started.

We're bike enthusiasts, as you've probably already guessed, but the project turned out to be much more of a challenge than we ever imagined. Before we signed the contracts with the publisher, we pictured ourselves tooling along leisurely, discovering new out-of-the-way paths by day, and eating gourmet meals by night. As the project got underway, though, we realized we'd left key elements out of our fantasies, things like flat tires, stopping along the way to write notes, getting totally lost and having to backtrack twenty miles in a gale-force headwind. Even now, from the perspective of several decades, we still agree it was the hardest work of our lives.

One day, chugging along cold and hungry about thirty miles from Alba in Northern Italy, we began to amuse ourselves by fantasizing about the bowl of minestrone we were going to have when we got to Alba. Exhausted and still with a couple of hours to go, we began using the minestrone as a motivator. Every few miles one of us would call out, "Tell me more about the minestrone!" If I were doing the description, I'd spin a long tale about the richness of the broth, the perfection of the spices, the freshness of the tomatoes, the warmth of the fireplace in front of which we'd be served, the crusty loaf of fresh-baked bread we'd dip into the soup, and any other detail that would help the miles go by. When it was Katie's turn, she'd take the minestrone into some higher stratosphere of magnificence. On we went, heads bent into the wind, driven forward by our quest for the ultimate minestrone.

Finally, in late afternoon we pedaled slowly into Alba. As we cruised down the main street, we searched right and left for the restaurant that would serve us the yearned-for soup. We passed one restaurant that looked absolutely perfect, but our pounding hearts sank when we saw that it wouldn't be open for an hour. Another one loomed up on the right. It looked wonderful, but the proprietors were just setting out the tables. They shook their heads—not open yet. By now we were nearly in tears. Suddenly fate or intuition or good luck intervened. We got the impulse to veer down a little side street. There, halfway down the block, was the restaurant of our fantasies, AND THE DOOR WAS OPEN! We screeched to a halt and practically fell over each other to get in the door. We were greeted by a most wonderful aroma of garlic, fresh-baking bread, and roasting chickens.

But NO! The staff members were all seated around a large table, having their own meal. The headwaiter, who turned out to be the only one who spoke a little English, came to us and humbly apologized that they were not quite open. "Give us just a half an hour," he said. "We are having our simple meal." We looked longingly at their "simple meal." You can probably guess what it was. It was a vast serving bowl of minestrone, accompanied by freshly baked loaves of bread. Several of the staff were so caught up in their enjoyment of it that they didn't even look up from their bowls.

We wanted that soup. We wanted it badly. We wanted it now.

Somehow, we must have transmitted the depth of forlornness to the headwaiter because he stepped back and regarded us with compassion bordering on pity. He held a finger aloft, then had a rapid-fire conversation with the staff, apparently appealing to them about our plight. He turned to us and said, "All we can offer you at the moment is our minestrone, but maybe it will make you happy until our chef can finish his meal." He lowered his voice gravely, "If he does not eat, he cannot cook."

We practically wept with gratitude. We bowed, we blew them kisses, we staggered to a table and removed our helmets and gloves. Soon, two large bowls of minestrone were set before us with a flourish. A warm loaf of bread came next, along with two glasses of rich, red Barolo. We thanked him profusely and took spoons in hand.

For the next half-hour, a soup-celebration was held in Alba, Italy. This was soup raised to the level of a sacrament. I kept asking Katie, a master chef, questions like "What is that spice?" and "How did they get tomatoes to taste like this?" Needless to say, it satisfied all our fantasies and then some. When our bowls were empty, we looked up at each other and made a decision: the quest ends here. This was it.

It's been many years since Alba, but sometimes in the winter I'll drop a broad hint or two. "Katie," I'll say. "Remember the Alba minestrone? Remember how wonderfully deep and hearty that broth was? Remember the way the beans were perfectly cooked and how it had those tiny bits of lean bacon in it? Remember how that soup seemed to nurture our very souls?"

A dreamy look will come over her as the memory takes hold. Next day, or maybe the day after that, I'll come into the kitchen and my nose will be greeted with the savory aroma of minestrone cooking on the stove. Katie, the miracle-woman in my life, the woman who can write books and talk on *Oprah* and operate an electric drill and grow prize-winning flowers, will be bringing another masterpiece of a soup to fruition. I'll taste it, and if I'm in an enlightened mood, I'll just savor it without even thinking of Alba. If I do think of Alba, I might say something like, "You know, honey, if I were the sort of guy who was into comparing your soup to that one we had in Alba, which I'm definitely not, I'd say yours might even be just a tiny bit better."

CHAPTER SIX

APPRECIATING THE CATS IN MY LIFE: LUCY, GRETA, AND ALI

I was a complete stranger to cats until I met Katie, a consummate cat-person. Since then, these remarkable beings have come to fascinate me more than I would ever have imagined. I've now had the privilege and joy of loving three cats, and in each case the experience has been life-changing.

One of the most precious relationships of my life was with our first cat, Lucy. We found each other in 1995, and from the moment she entered our lives she was pure joy. Lucy was with us for almost eighteen years until she died in our arms in 2012. Lucy had so much presence and such a refined consciousness that I never really thought of her as a pet. She was a treasured companion who came into my life by grace, a teacher who helped me see more clearly how life really works.

Lucy came to us in a magic moment. We decided to get a cat as a Christmas present to ourselves in 1995, our first year in Santa Barbara. We lived at the time just a couple of blocks away from a pet shop on the main street of Montecito. Passing by the shop one day we saw a beautiful gray Persian reclining majestically in the window. She was so captivatingly regal that we went inside to take a closer look. Frances, the cat with the queenly presence, was the owner's pride and joy, and she was DEFINITELY not for sale, said the owner with an indignant glare. However, we found that Frances had recently delivered what was to be her last litter. There were five kittens, and if we came back in two weeks, they would be ready for adoption. The owner named an exorbitant price, and when she saw my surprise, she wagged her finger and said the price was non-negotiable. I had never bought a cat before; in my mind getting a cat was something you did by donating ten bucks at an animal shelter. Not so in Montecito, California. Still, we couldn't get Frances off our minds, so two weeks later we went back to the shop to see the kittens.

We went downstairs into the basement room where they were playing. We stood quietly by the door watching five madcap bundles of gray fur ricocheting around the room. One of them, a big male, actually crashed into my legs, picked himself up and dashed off again. In a moment, though, a bit of magic happened. A petite girl-kitten came jogging over to us, took a seat on her haunches and looked up at us with the clearest gaze and the sweetest face we'd ever seen. Katie and I both laughed out loud and felt our hearts melt.

"Looks like we found our kitten," I said.

"Or she found us," Katie said.

I reached down and scooped her up gently.

Suddenly the price seemed irrelevant, a bargain even. We took Lucy up the road to her new home, and thus began our lives together. A definitive event occurred the first night Lucy was with us. We'd been playing with her non-stop all evening, during which she occasionally collapsed in a heap for a catnap. By bedtime, Katie and I were exhausted. We got Lucy settled in her little cat-bed and went off to collapse into our own bed. We dropped off to sleep right away, but in the middle of the night I woke up, aware of another presence in our bed. I looked over and saw one of most charming sights I've ever seen in my life. Lucy had gotten under the covers between us, with her tiny head sticking out just like our heads. And that's the way it was for the many more thousands of nights she was with us. After we went to sleep every night, Lucy would slip in between us and spend the rest of the night there.

Lucy had a very refined consciousness. One day I was working with a couple in my home office. Lucy was napping on the bed in our master bedroom, down a long hall from the office. Because nobody else was home, I'd left the door to the rest of the house open. As the session progressed, the woman began to access some deep memories and feelings rooted in her experience as a Holocaust survivor.

She began to shake and quiver, as people often do when they're feeling the emergence of old fears, grief, and anger. Part of us wants to let go and part of us wants to hold on, resulting in a hesitant shudder like you get when one foot is on the accelerator and the other on the brakes. I was about to suggest to the woman that she take a few deep breaths to help her relax into the feelings, but before I got the words out of my mouth, Lucy strode purposefully into the room. She immediately trotted over to the woman and snuggled her sturdy body up against the woman's leg. The woman looked down, saw Lucy, and burst into tears. Her resistance melted and all her old feelings poured forth. Lucy stood right by her for the next ten minutes, as the woman let go of a lifetime's burden of unexpressed feelings.

Finally, the wave of intense emotion crested and began to subside. The woman looked around the room in wonderment, as if reborn. Lucy sensed the change, because she looked up at the woman and quietly withdrew from the room. After the session, I looked in the bedroom and saw Lucy asleep again in her spot on the bed.

On another occasion, I was sitting cross-legged on my bed, typing on my laptop computer. From where I sat, I could see out to the backyard, where Lucy was roaming around. Lost in my writer's trance, I became aware of an insistent scratching on the screen door, so I got up to let Lucy in. When I got to the door, I saw that Lucy had something in her jaws. It was a live hummingbird, fluttering wildly to get away. Lucy had brought me a few such "gifts" before, but her captured prey had always been mice. I freaked out at seeing the poor little hummingbird frantically trying to get out of Lucy's jaw. I fell to my knees to pry Lucy's jaws open.

I saw the look of confusion in Lucy's eyes as I tried to get her mouth open with my fingers. No doubt she thought she was doing me a favor by bringing me the little bird. The more I tried to open her jaws the harder she clamped down, frozen between her nature and her desire to please me. Suddenly I realized that my attempts to save the little bird might have the opposite result, so I let go of Lucy and gave her some space. She was locked in eye contact with me, as if awaiting further instructions, but I saw that I had been trying to communicate with her in a primitive way. An inspiration came to me.

In my mind I gave Lucy a silent appreciation that went something like this: "I honor you for being such a good hunter. I'd also appreciate it if you'd let the bird go." In my mind I sent Lucy a telepathic picture of her opening her jaws and letting the bird go.

A split-second later Lucy opened her jaws and let the bird fly free. It zipped off to a nearby tree limb to recover. I picked up Lucy and gave her a good cuddle. I thanked her profusely and took her into the kitchen for a little treat.

I learned a lot in that moment about how to work with people. From that day forward, I made sure I honored people for the survival programs that had gotten them to where they were, even if those same survival programs were choking the life out of them and those around them. Honoring their old programs helped them let go of them so that they could enjoy the love available to them in the present. I also learned to communicate better with people in pictures as well as words. I learned that most of us are gripping the hummingbird of life too tightly, simply because of our ancient programming, and that well-meaning people around us are trying to get us to let go by prying too hard.

When I get stuck, that moment with Lucy helps me lighten up my grip, honor the survival-beast inside me, and let my hummingbird soar free.

Greta and Ali

After Lucy's death we took a year to mourn her passing; during that time, we breathed our way through many waves of sadness. Several people encouraged us to get another cat right away, but that didn't feel right. It felt unfair to a new cat to bring her into our lives just to assuage our grief. One day, though, Katie and I looked at each other and realized it was time to open our hearts to a new cat. I spotted a couple of British Shorthair cats on a Facebook video and was instantly smitten with their Cheshire Cat look. We did some research and found that one of the premier breeders of British Shorthairs was less than an hour from us. As it happened, her prize cat, Abby, had just delivered a litter, including two sisters who looked like identical twins. When it came time for them to be adopted, we introduced the two girls to their new home, where they have lived happily ever since. As this is being written, Greta and Ali have been with us a little over seven years and have become cherished companions.

Ali is very athletic, loves to jump into boxes, and climb on things. She loves to cuddle and has the deepest, richest purr I've ever heard. Greta is quiet, thoughtful, and has a healing instinct. I hurt my left knee a few years back and ended up having a total knee replacement. The day I got home from the hospital, I fell into bed and got my leg arranged so it didn't hurt. No sooner had I gotten comfortable than Greta jumped up on the bed and snuggled up against my left knee. She rested her head on exactly the place it was most tender, and there she stayed for a good hour.

We sat down with Greta and Ali early on in their lives to tell them about Lucy. We wanted them to know about the space of love they were coming into, the atmosphere we'd created with Lucy over the years she was with us. We also wanted to reassure them that they weren't there to replace Lucy, but to be their own special selves. They responded magnificently and in their grown-up years have become two of the most sensitive, loving beings you could imagine.

I was fifty years old before I experienced the special magic of loving a pet, but now I can't imagine living without that sweet feeling. I'm feeling it especially intensely right now, having just given Greta a good brushing, which she loves, and tickled Ali behind the ears as I passed by.

(PS: Readers who want to see Greta and Ali in action can find a treasure trove on Instagram, @hendricks.gay)

CHAPTER SEVEN

ADVENTURES IN NON-ORDINARY STATES OF CONSCIOUSNESS

I've meditated every day since 1972, morning and evening, so the non-ordinary consciousness I most enjoy now is the clear, serene, no-thought state meditation creates. I've written in other books about my experiences with meditation, so in this chapter I focus on the non-ordinary consciousness produced by psychoactive medicines of various kinds.

The first time I remember encountering consciousness-altering medicines was in a magazine article I read in high school. It described a journey into a remote section of Mexico, where the journalist took psychedelic mushrooms and described his visions. The article also had pictures of the ancient female shaman that led him through his trips. I found it absolutely riveting and vowed on the spot to have those kinds of adventures myself. It would take a couple of decades, but I would eventually come to have my own adventures with peyote and other consciousness-expanding medicines in the far reaches of Mexico.

In college, my roommate and I grew a couple of pot plants, but they turned out to be fairly puny specimens. The buds did little to alter my consciousness besides inspiring me to devour an immoderate amount of brownies and vanilla ice cream.

If my weed was a dud, my first LSD experience was anything but. It made a powerful, positive impression on me that continues to resonate in my life. One Saturday in Palo Alto, c. 1970, I took a dose of blotter acid and stretched out on my bed to await the effects. I hadn't planned to record my trip, but as the effects came on, I noticed my cassette recorder nearby. I clicked it on and was able to capture 45 minutes of my excursion. For the first 15 minutes, all you can hear on the tape is my heavy, slow breathing, often with an audible long "Ah" on the out-breath. Finally, I speak my first words, in a breathy whisper of awe-struck wonder: "There's a web that connects everything in the world!" Then I go back to my breathing and my ever-longer "Ah."

Another 15 minutes go by, then I speak my final words on the tape. Again, in my breathy wonder-voice, I say "I'm going to call it the Web of the World!" Then I realize it doesn't matter what I call it and lapse off into laughter, sighs of delight, and then more breathing. From that space, I felt another truth emerge, seeming to come from my body rather than my mind: we make our way through the Web of the World by loving the things we encounter. Our progress through the world is determined by how much love we can give and receive.

Fifty years and many thousands of clients later, I value the truth of that insight more than ever.

I remember the next day as vividly as the trip itself. I could feel my connection to the world around me in a way I never had before. I remember pausing to examine flowers on a bush and realizing they were essentially the same thing as me but arranged in a different way. I also felt the same connection of oneness with people I passed by. I saw that others were the same as me but wearing a different skin-suit. I saw that below the surface we all have the same emotions, the same wiring, and the same essential humanness. That was how I felt after that first LSD trip, and I've felt that way ever since.

My mentor in the world of transformational medicine was a sprightly elder, Dr. Leo Zeff. Through him I got to meet other pioneers of the field such as Alexander "Sasha" Shulgin, Ralph Metzner, and others. I met Timothy Leary a couple of times but never resonated with him, partly due to his ever-present cigarette. Like many reformed addicts, I'm a bit of a zealot on the subject. He also drank alcohol in a way that I didn't enjoy being around. I admired his writings, but in person we weren't a good fit.

From 1980 to 1986 I sampled Leo's full medicine bag, including psilocybin mushrooms, LSD, ayahuasca, ibogaine, MDA, 2CB, and MDMA. All my experiences were done in the special context Leo created, a spiritual journey of deep exploration. As a result, I never had a bad trip or saw anyone else have one. In those same years, I also did one ketamine trip administered by a psychiatrist friend, and a wild 15-minute ride on what is now called 5-MEO.

Ayahuasca has gotten very popular in recent years, but when I took it in the mid-80s I didn't know much about it. One Sunday afternoon, I took the medicine and sat back to await its onset. After an hour or so I began to have an irresistible urge to crawl around on the floor emitting low, growling sounds. It just seemed like the thing to do. Soon, I was in full jungle-cat mode, moving stealthily across the floor making deeply satisfying throaty roars. After a few roars, I realized that if I got the sound of my roar harmonized with the vibrational frequency of the inner buzz I was feeling, I got transported into an ecstatic new space that was beyond vibration. In that space, it was as if I could look down through my energy body and see precisely the places I was still stuck. From that perspective, I saw something that changed my life profoundly.

I realized I'd always seen the world from a male perspective. That was natural, of course, but in my state of heightened awareness I saw how it was a severe limitation. It was blocking out a whole other way of looking at life. I remember thinking something like "I wonder what it's like to see things from a woman's point of view." Next thing I knew I was in a tropical jungle teeming with joyful life bursting out everywhere. It didn't stop there, though.

As I let go further into the ayahuasca visions, I became aware of an immense collective pain associated with being a woman. I had a rush of images that seemed to come out of deep places in my body—women being persecuted by stoning and burned as witches, Joan of Arc, women being beaten by their mates. The deeper I breathed into my body, the faster the images came. It was if I'd somehow stored in my own body the collective pain women had endured for thousands of years. Then, a deeper awareness opened up: ALL men had those same feelings stored in us—we'd just turned our back on them for thousands of years.

The next insight was equally compelling. I realized that the hope of humanity—perhaps our only hope—lay in men's ability to befriend the energy of the feminine, to listen to women and honor their wisdom. As I felt my way down into the soul-level depths of myself, I realized that honoring the feminine was one of the essential paths of my life. It was part of my mission. Best of all, I had the perfect place to practice my new awareness sitting next to me, holding space for my journey! Katie was almost always the space-holder for my explorations, and there she was, in the full, radiant glory of her femininity. I remember lying on my back for a long time, opening my awareness to what it must feel like to be her, to be that exquisitely sensitive, to feel connected to the moon and the pull of the tides.

The ayahuasca experience made a difference in our relationship. Afterwards, I was able to resonate with Katie's feelings in a new way. Instead of trying to talk her out of whatever she was feeling, such as anger or sadness, I simply tuned into her feelings and listened to her tell me about them. 99% of the time, that was all I needed to do. Since childhood, I'd spent a lot of energy trying to "fix" women when they were upset, usually trying to get them to be less emotional and see the world more logically. My mother was usually frantically busy; she ran on two packs of unfiltered Camels and a dozen cups of coffee a day. As a result, she could go into rage at the drop of a fork. I can't count the number of times I talked her down from whatever she was fuming about. On that ayahuasca journey I realized what a stupid enterprise it was to think I could teach women anything. Ayahuasca showed me that my path was to listen to women, to resonate with the feminine, and appreciate the mystery.

Another story from that era: one day in 1980 Leo called, telling me with great excitement about a new discovery, MDMA. He urged Katie and me both to take it, suggesting that she sit with me while I took it and vice-versa. The following Sunday afternoon, I took the medicine and stretched out on a thick pad, with Katie cross-legged on a cushion next to me. After a while I began to feel vibrations in my body, accompanied by a warm feeling inside. At first the vibrations felt a little rough, and Katie pointed out that it looked like I was resisting. As soon as she said that, I let go and the medicine came on. With that particular chemical, you're either turned on or you're not; the moment you turn on you're as turned on as you're going to be for the next hour until it peaks and starts to fade. I met Katie's loving gaze and felt my cells expand to become wide-open love receptors. For the next four hours I reveled in love ... for Katie, for myself, for the world with all its treasures and sorrows.

Of all the experiences during my psychedelic era, one memory warms my heart more than perhaps any other. Thanks to Leo, who had made the journey before me, I was invited one year to join a group of indigenous people on a trek to the peyote fields of the Mexican desert. They were mainly members of the Huichol tribe, with a few from the neighboring Cora tribe.

The Huichol village is near Tepic, just up the road from the seaside resort of Puerto Vallarta. Wirikuti, their ancient name for the tiny place where the peyote grows, is several hundred miles away in the central desert beyond San Luis Potosi. In ancient days, the journey to the desert was always made on foot over several weeks, accompanied by ceremonies along the way. In modern Mexico, cattle ranchers have taken over much of the land, stringing up hundreds of fences that make a foot journey impossible. On my trip, we took a succession of smaller buses all the way from Tepic to Charcas, on the edge of the desert. The rest of the journey was on the back of a flatbed truck, with all of us hanging on for dear life as we bounced along the rutted track into the desert.

We set up camp around the big tree that distinguishes Wirikuti. I should say "they set up camp," because I'm hopelessly un-mechanical and easily stymied by complex items like tent-pegs. Also, since we're on the subject of camping, I should confess a secret known only to my closest friends and family: I loathe camping. However, on this occasion, all the discomforts—freezing nights, blazing hot days, tents collaps-ing on top of us in a midnight gale—were all made worthwhile by one bite of roasted corn.

Let me explain.

The first day we spent most of the morning hunting for peyote. It's a little, round cactus that grows close to the ground and is notoriously hard to spot. I spent my first hour shuffling along, staring down at the desert floor trying unsuccessfully to spot a peyote cactus among the other clumps of vegetation. The shaman noticed my frustration and came over to whisper in my ear: "You need to get on the cactus's wavelength. Just feel what it must feel like to be a juicy little thing living in a desert, something that's makes people high and happy."

I relaxed into that attitude and got rewarded for it right away. I spotted a cactus not a yard from where I was standing. I got down on my belly and lowered my head to the ground. I wanted to see what the world looked like from the cactus' point of view. Suddenly I could see them everywhere, almost as if they were winking at me. There were at least a dozen of them within ten feet of where I'd been standing. I picked all I was likely to need and went back to camp to get the shaman's blessing for my trip.

I don't remember much about the actual content of that first peyote journey, just an overall impression of opening a new space in my mind that I called "the celestial canopy." I remember something that didn't happen, though! Along the way to getting people stoned, peyote is famously known to make them vomit. The shaman told us that it only did so to the extent that you needed cleaning out. He said if you'd been living a toxic life, the medicine had to clean you out before it could do its healing work. Thanks to my health-conscious wife, Katie, I eat an extremely refined diet of mostly organic food. The peyote never gave me slightest gastric discomfort, in contrast to some of the other adventurers. When one of the indigenous men got violently sick, the shaman told him it was because he'd been living in the city eating fast foods. Between groans, the sufferer immediately confirmed the shaman's diagnosis.

That evening around the campfire, the shaman offered us another exotic medicine, dried toad-foam excreted by a psychedelic frog. It contained DMT, a psychedelic that only lasted 15 minutes or so and was said to produce quite a ride. Of course, I was first to raise my hand. The shaman offered me a pipe and lit the weird-smelling powder. I took a few puffs and WHOOSH! The next thing I knew, I was stretched out on my back with my hands high above my head, receiving a ecstatic freight-train rush of energy coursing up through my body and taking me out into space.

"Toad," as the shaman called the medicine, turned out to be a very short hop. One moment I was on my back, immersed in the far reaches of space, the pure consciousness beyond thoughts, feelings, and body sensations. A few minutes later, I was back to the now, appreciating the brilliant array of stars above me in the desert night, hearing the crackle of the fire and the soft conversations of my comrades in the circle around me. As I was sitting up again, the shaman came over, bowed to me and said, "Toad likes you."

"I like Toad," I said, to the great merriment of the others around the fire.

One final piece of magic happened that evening. Only three more participants elected to take Toad's wild ride, and after they finished, we turned our attention to dinner. It was an unusual one, only two courses: a huge pot of oatmeal mixed with brown sugar, and corn that had been roasted in its husk. A tiny woman, a Huichol elder, was in charge of food and as I later learned, on a quest to heal cancer in her body. She took the charred pieces of corn out of the fire and handed them around. I'd never had corn roasted whole like that, but when I took my first bite, I became a convert. The smoky taste, with some of kernels burnt and caramelized, was a savory departure from anything I'd ever tasted. I grew up in the Deep South, where corn on the cob has virtual religious status, but it was always steamed or part of a crab boil. I'd never seen it roasted directly on the coals. Since then, Katie and I have served corn on the cob at dozens of backyard barbecues, with nary a boiled one on the menu. Sometimes our guests' eyes widen when they get a piece of corn, whole in its scorched husk, plopped on their plate. A moment later, though, I'm guaranteed to see a big smile on their faces when they take their first bite.

It's been many years since I've taken consciousness-expanding medicines, so it's fitting that we end a chapter on altered states of consciousness with a paean to roasted corn. I learned a lot from the medicines and appreciate them immensely, but as the old saying goes, "Once you get the message, hang up the phone." I realized ultimately that the medicines only point the way; the real work is to integrate the medicine's inspiration into daily life. At my current stage of life (77 years old as I write these words in early 2022), the ordinary realities of my life are medicine enough for me. My life over the past few decades has been like one long bite of roasted sweet corn. The flow of love in my relationship with Katie is a constant, beautiful presence in my consciousness. The home we've created, the body of work we teach, our community of friends around the world—all that richness is a blessing beyond anything I ever imagined.

CHAPTER EIGHT

VERY SMALL MEETINGS WITH VERY BIG PEOPLE: CHANCE ENCOUNTERS WITH ELVIS PRESLEY AND JIMI HENDRIX

I grew up with radio, not television. There was plenty of television around, black and white in those days, but just not in my house. My mother was staunchly opposed to the new invention. She took a look at people's fascination with it and concluded that it would ultimately destroy family life and cause the decline of civilization. She was probably right, but I found her position infuriating at the time. If I wanted to see any of the popular shows of the era, such as Steve Allen or Ed Sullivan, I had to go up the block to my aunt's house. Many of the references my peers made—to Beaver Cleaver, Howdy Doody and 77 Sunset Strip—were completely lost on me.

My mother thought radio was okay, probably because she had grown up with it in the Roaring Twenties. We had a big wooden Philco radio in the living room; I also had a small one in my bedroom. The little radio had the tinniest speakers I've ever heard. One possible reason: a friend of mine who had the same model took his apart after it stopped working, only to discover that the metal inside the radio still had a Budweiser label on it! The enterprising Japanese had built it out of recycled beer cans.

9 p.m. was bedtime, but in the sixth grade I started listening furtively to *Spinner Sanctum*, which came on at 10 p.m. with the top ten songs of the day. *Spinner Sanctum* was where I got my first taste of the new music called rock 'n roll. I remember pressing my ear to the radio to hear "Rock Around the Clock" and "See You Later, Alligator" by Bill Haley and The Comets. I remember loving anything by The Platters or Chuck Berry. And it was on *Spinner Sanctum* that I first heard the voice of Elvis Presley.

Elvis changed everything. There was something about Elvis that was special, different, more vivid somehow than anything else I heard on the radio. I scraped up enough money to buy the first Elvis album, the one with "Heartbreak Hotel," "Don't Be Cruel," and "I Got a Woman." I must have played that record five hundred times, savoring every little nuance of Elvis' unique style. If you want to hear the essence of rock 'n roll, listen to the first few seconds of "I Got a Woman" on that album. The very first sound Elvis makes on that song, when he groans "Way-uhl" instead of "Well," conveys the entire underlying attitude that makes rock so captivating.

For a couple of weeks, I went around the house bellowing out "Way-uhl" about fifty times a day, driving my mother and brother nuts. My fascination with Elvis grew and grew, though, and when I was in the seventh grade, I heard rumors of something even more wonderful: Elvis was coming to Orlando to play a concert.

Orlando was the only large city near the sleepy little hamlet I grew up in. It was just forty miles away, but it seemed like a different planet from the town where my family had lived since the early 1900s. I could hardly believe that the Actual, Real Elvis Presley was going to come to Orlando. Finally, I determined that the rumor was true, and set my sights on getting to that concert any way I could.

If my mother was opposed to television, you can imagine how she felt about Elvis Presley and the whole phenomenon of rock 'n roll. She loathed him. Indeed, she saw him as the incarnation of the devil, as did many of the "respectable" folks in the South of that era. It didn't help when Jerry Lee Lewis actually came out and said rock was "the Devil's music."

"See," my mother said, pointing to the newspaper article quoting Jerry Lee, "they admit it themselves."

Clever lad that I was, I hit upon a winning strategy for getting to the concert. My mother was a newspaper columnist and reporter, so I sold her on the idea of getting press passes to the concert so she could interview Elvis. To my amazement, she thought this was a good idea, so she requested and got a press pass to interview Elvis, along with two free tickets. I would not be allowed to go with her backstage to interview Elvis before the show, but at least I would be able to be in the audience. As the day of the concert approached, I virtually vibrated with excitement. The fact that the concert coincided with my twelfth birthday gave it an even bigger charge.

Finally, the day arrived, and we made the trek to Orlando in my mother's blue Plymouth station wagon, with me praying all the way that it wouldn't pick this day to stage one of its frequent breakdowns. We parked at the Orlando Municipal Auditorium and went inside, where my mother was ushered off backstage with a number of other journalists to await Elvis' arrival. The concert was still hours away, so I went outside and found a shady spot in a park behind the auditorium. I spread out the homework I'd brought to work on, as part of the deal I'd made with my mother to be allowed to go to a concert on a school night. After a while the light began to fade, so I put my books away and began wandering around the deserted park, just killing time until the doors officially opened at 7 p.m. A huge crowd had gathered in front of the auditorium, but around behind the building where the park was located, there was nobody else but me. The auditorium was hidden behind a row of oak trees and wasn't visible from the park.

Suddenly something caught my attention. From far up the street, I saw a line of white Cadillacs cruising slowly toward me. I saw that the driver of the lead Cadillac was craning his neck out the window, obviously looking for a landmark. My whole body snapped to attention: it had to be Elvis and his entourage! Nobody but Elvis could afford half a dozen Cadillacs, a car that was even rumored to have air conditioning in it! To a kid growing up in the muggy heat of Central Florida, riding around in your own little bubble of air conditioning was like having your own spaceship.

I rushed over to the curb to get a closer look, hoping to catch a glimpse of The Great One as he went into the auditorium. My excitement turned to frozen terror, though, when the line of Cadillacs rolled to a stop a few feet away from me. The automatic window glided down, and Elvis Presley leaned his head out the passenger-side window.

"Hey boy," The King said, in his famous Memphis mumble. "You know where the Orlando Municipal Auditorium is?"

My jaw locked into a wide-open expression of total astonishment. I tried to get my mouth to form words, but my jaw was so thoroughly frozen that all I could manage was a couple of guttural grunts. Finally, I gave up trying to speak and, zombie-like, slowly raised my arm to point to the back of the large building behind the trees.

Elvis, recognizing my condition, gave me a grin and a wink. "Thank'ya very much," he said, as the window glided back up again. The cars eased off toward the parking lot, leaving me trembling in the wake of destiny.

I don't remember much about the concert except that it was hard to hear Elvis over the screams of the teenage girls. However, I would bask in the memory of my curbside encounter for the rest of my life. It was not only a meeting with a hero, it was an early moment of discovering the power of manifestation: I could make things happen if I got creative and focused my single-minded attention on it.

As to my mother's interview, it pretty much conformed to her expectations. She found Elvis polite but pronounced his music "vulgar." There was no convincing her otherwise from then on. In defense of Elvis, there was no convincing my mother otherwise about much of anything. In addition to the usual parent-like certainty of her rightness, she also had the added weight of being paid for her opinions and having them displayed every day on the front page. In short, she was hard to argue with, although that didn't stop me from trying on a regular basis throughout my teenage years.

It seems like every generation has to come up with a thing or two that the previous generation can't stand. My mother cringed at my Elvis records, just as I cringed at some of my daughter's pop music in the early '80s. Fortunately, Amanda also had a taste for some of my favorites such as Hendrix, Bob Marley, and The Specials. These days, lots of parents are probably cringing at their children's hip-hop. On it goes, across the great divide.

In the '60s I had the opportunity to meet a number of prominent musicians and attend dozens of great concerts. In all those experiences one other great moment stands out: meeting Jimi Hendrix and hearing his music for the first time.

I was a disc jockey at WLOF in Orlando in 1967, working full-time and going to college part-time. At the time, The Monkees were a hot band, thanks to a television show that ran for a couple of seasons. As part of the promotion for the concert, we had a big contest to give away 100 free tickets. The radio station paid me an extra $50 to chaperone one of the two busloads of winners to The Monkees concert in Jacksonville. I wasn't looking forward to it, seeing as how everybody but the driver and me was under fifteen years old. I also wasn't looking forward to enduring an hour of Monkees music. For those born in the post-Monkees era, you may not know this band and how it came into being. It was the brainchild of a couple of television producers, who decided to create a band and a TV show specifically for the thirteen-year-old set. They were wildly popular for a couple of years, then dropped like a rock off the screen and the charts.

A week before the concert, we got a piece of news that would change my attitude radically. Jimi Hendrix, the new guitar phenomenon we were just beginning to hear about, had been tapped to be the opening act! In other words, the band I most wanted to see was opening for the band I least wanted to see.

It had to be the strangest pairing in rock history. Hendrix was the new psychedelic guitar hero. What was he doing with The Monkees? I found that it was a pairing arranged by the record label that only lasted for a handful of shows. I feel incredibly lucky that I got to be at one of them.

On the night of the concert, I dutifully escorted my charges into the Coliseum and got them seated. I started down the aisle toward the backstage door, where I was supposed to have my picture taken with The Monkees. About halfway down the aisle, though, Hendrix and his two mates ambled out onto the stage to play their set. I hunkered down right on the spot to hear what they sounded like.

Their sound felt like it rearranged my brain cells. I had never heard anything like it in my life. It wasn't just the massive stack of Marshall amplifiers behind him. Jimi was getting sounds out of his Flying-V guitar that I didn't know it could make. Halfway through the set, it suddenly dawned on me that he was left-handed, playing a right-handed guitar upside-down. I was transfixed (and still am. Hardly a week goes by without putting on headphones and listening to some Hendrix.)

The audience was largely made up of pre-teen and teen-age girls, many of whom were accompanied by their mothers. They politely applauded after every song, but I also saw some of the girls in the audience looking at each other with eye-rolls and those "gag-me-with-a-spoon" expressions they're famous for. Probably as a result of this tepid reception, Jimi played a very short set of twenty minutes or so. I remained transfixed throughout. When they finished, I hurried backstage so I could meet him.

I was first to greet him when he came down the ramp. I shouted over the din, "That was the greatest music I've ever heard in my life."

"Hey, man, thanks," he said. He awkwardly stuck out his hand and I pumped it wildly. (In later years, I reflected often on the feel of his hand. It was soft, like touching a cloud. I think I expected his fingers to be tough and calloused from playing the way he did, but they were baby soft.) I told him I wanted to interview him on the radio the next afternoon and he told me the hotel where he'd be down in Miami. I told him I'd call the next afternoon at 4 p.m.

The next afternoon I called Jimi at the appointed time, and after many rings heard a sleepy "Hullo."

"Did I wake you up?" I asked.

"Umm, yeah. What time is it?"

"4 p.m.," I said. "Should I call back later?"

"No, man, it's okay. I gotta get up anyway."

I wish I had a tape of our brief interview, because I don't remember much about what we talked about. It was 'live' on the air on a Sunday afternoon in 1967, so I suspect some fan somewhere has it for sale on the Internet. The one thing I remember was asking him what it was like to be on the strange bill with The Monkees.

He said, "Well, it's just somethin' I gotta do."

A bizarre footnote to this story: thirty-five years later in Ojai, California, I went over to play a round of golf at the course in my neighborhood, the Ojai Valley Inn. My golfing partner, Tom Boyer, and I were asked if a solo golfer could join us. It turned out to be Mickey Dolenz, drummer for the Monkees! When I shook his hand, I told him that I had shaken it once before in 1967. Astonished, he asked me where it was.

"I'll give you a hint," I said. "I shook the hand of Jimi Hendrix the same night."

He just smiled and shook his head in wonderment.

CHAPTER NINE

THE MANY JOBS I'VE HAD

Katie says I've had more jobs than anyone she's ever met. I've certainly had more jobs than anyone I've ever met. For as long as I can remember I've liked setting up enterprises, beginning in elementary school, when I borrowed Mom's card table and launched my first lemonade stand. It was an utter flop. I learned firsthand that location is everything and that flies love lemonade. Nobody came by my stand, all my ice melted, and I trudged back home without selling a single cup. There's also a family story that I drank up my inventory, but if that happened, I've conveniently forgotten it.

Next came my egg business. My mother developed a back-to-the-land fantasy when I was about ten years old. My brother had just escaped to college, so I became the actual executioner of the fantasy. She bought 50 chickens, the limit that was allowed within the city, and put me in charge of everything from collecting the eggs to dispatching chickens for Sunday dinner. My big reward was that every Saturday I got to take eggs around the neighborhood in my red wagon, selling them for fifty cents a dozen to regular customers. Two disasters ended the egg business and Mom's back-to-the-land fantasy.

Disaster #1 was when the chickens escaped through a hole in the fence and went into the neighbor's backyard, there to feast on berries that littered the ground. Unfortunately, the berries were from a camphor tree. For the next week or two all the eggs tasted and smelled like Vicks VapoRub. After the camphor was out of their systems I returned to my Saturday rounds, only to incur a heartbreaking second disaster. I was lugging a dozen eggs up the steps to Mrs. Geiger's house when I tripped and fell, crushing the eggs under me. I barked my shin, too, bad enough to make me cry. I can still remember picking myself up off the steps, gooey eggs all over the front of me, and skulking back home in shame. Mom ended up giving all the chickens to a friend who lived on a farm outside town.

When I was in the third grade, a circus came to town and set up in an open field near my house. I went over to watch them put up the tent and got into a conversation with the man who took care of the animals. He must have spotted my enterprising nature because he offered me a job watering the elephants. He offered me a dime a day, a sum that left me virtually speechless with gratitude. I would have happily watered the elephants for free; getting paid for it was a gift from the gods. I didn't tell my mother about the new job for a few days. The circus employees I was hanging around were exactly the kind of people mothers warn their kids not to hang around. By the time Mom caught on, my job had evolved from merely watering the elephants to shoveling out their massive excretions. I'd negotiated an extra nickel a day for my services, so when I got busted at least I had a fist full of nickels and dimes to show Mom. On the fateful day, Mom noticed a distinctive smell about me when I trooped in from work. She said, "What on earth have you been doing?"

I told her about my new job and the raise I'd gotten after my first day. I also announced that I was thinking of dropping out of elementary school to go on the road with the circus. By then, my mother was used to my overheated enthusiasms, so she took it in stride and said we would discuss it later. She didn't have to worry, though. The circus was in town for five days, and after five days of wielding my bucket and shovel I had pretty much lost my fascination for the circus life. Ever since then, my dealings with elephant poop have been purely metaphorical.

My family owned a six-acre orange grove about ten miles outside Leesburg. It also had a couple of acres of bare ground that my mother tried growing other things on, including watermelons and cotton. One of my early jobs was helping out with whatever harvest was going on. I picked cotton for a few days, which is a particularly unpleasant job involving hot sun, cotton bolls that prick your fingers, and a giant burlap sack you drag along behind you to put the cotton in. However, it gives me lifetime bragging rights. Once when my daughter was about ten years old, I was telling her the story of my brief career as a cotton-picker. She listened carefully, then cocked her head and said, "Daddy, did that actually happen?" "Yep, Amanda, that actually happened."

The watermelon harvest was brutal, too, because it occurred at peak of summer, with 95-degree days steaming with 95% humidity. The first day I got assigned to pick the watermelons off the vine and lug them down to the end of the row. Another kid was stationed there to hoist them onto the truck when it came around. As I hauled melons along the rows in the broiling sun, I began to envy the other kid's job. It looked a lot easier just standing there until the truck came along. In the afternoon, taking refuge from the tropical downpour that usually occurred around 2 p.m., I asked the boss what I had to do to get the other kid's cushy job.

He laughed. "You want it? You can have it. Hey, Bobby, you work the rows for a while. Let Gay work the truck."

We switched places and I started my coveted new job. Within an hour I desperately wanted my old one back. Every time the truck rolled up, I had about five minutes to hoist fifty watermelons up onto the truck. By quitting time, my back was screaming with pain. Fortunately, my watermelon-picking career was even shorter than my three days as a cotton-picker; it only took us a couple of days to pick the field clean.

I scored my first marketing coup with my next enterprise. It was the summer after fifth grade, so I would have been ten going on eleven. My next-door neighbor, Sam Lewin, was a watermelon merchant about seventy years old at the time. I often chatted with him when I'd see him across the hedge; I think he got a kick out of talking to me because I was always peppering him with questions about business. His own kids were doctors and lawyers who lived in New York, where Mr. Lewin spent half the year.

One day I made a business proposition to him. I offered to buy four watermelons from him at wholesale, which in those days was fifteen cents a melon. My plan was to take the melons down the hill to Highway 27, a couple hundred yards away, and hawk them to passing motorists for twenty-five cents apiece. I would pocket a dime profit on each melon, a virtual windfall. In a world where gas was twenty-five cents a gallon, dimes were a much more highly valued item than they are now. At Carney's drug store I could get a soda-fountain Pepsi for a nickel.

The first day, I held my sign up every time a car passed, "Watermelon! 25 Cents!" There was plenty of traffic, but nobody stopped. I didn't sell a single melon and had to haul all four of them back up the hill. That night, though, I was seized by inspiration: cut each melon into eight pieces and sell the pieces for a nickel each! That way, I'd be making an astronomical profit of a quarter a melon instead of a dime! The next day I held a beautiful red slice of melon up to the motorists instead of a sign. Boom! Instant marketing gold.

It was a roasting hot day, which also worked to my advantage. Many drivers actually slammed on their brakes when they spotted me holding those juicy slices of melon aloft. I sold all four melons in under an hour, with one motorist buying ten slices for a large family crammed in a station wagon. Even with my demo slices and a couple I ate myself, I made $1.50 against my original investment of sixty cents. I took my red wagon back up the hill and negotiated for more melons, selling out again in less than an hour. I went up and down the hill all day until sundown. When I finally went home, I was tired and desperately in need of a shower, but I had almost $4 in my pocket. I felt like a millionaire.

For a short while I also mowed lawns, but I messed up the edging on my uncle's lawn and got fired. I'm always looking for ways to turn adversity into possibility, though, so out of getting fired I hatched a better idea. I hired a couple of neighborhood kids to operate the lawn mower for fifty cents an hour, then sold their services at a rate that allowed me to pocket about a dollar an hour. This gave me a taste of the marvelous concept of leverage, although I wouldn't learn that word until a couple of decades later.

My career as a lawn broker sputtered to a halt when my mother, a soul of strict moral principle, discovered what I was doing and busted me. Her grounds were that I was taking advantage of kids who were not as cognitively gifted as I was. That was certainly true, but I argued that I was giving the kids a way to make a little money instead of just sitting around.

Plus, nobody was complaining about the deal. However, like everybody else who ever tried to argue with Mom, I failed to convince her and was out of the lawn business.

Other than picking cotton and watermelons, my brief career as a bowling alley pinsetter was probably my worst job. Bowling isn't very popular now, but if you were around in the 1950s, you lived through one of the biggest leisure-time crazes in our history. Suddenly, new bowling alleys were popping up everywhere—clean, air-conditioned, and automated. Soon, almost everybody on my block was in a bowling league. Every Saturday morning my friends and I would troop off to the bowling alley to compete against the other leagues. It was a great place to meet up with girls, too. My first girlfriend, Maureen McHale, came from the bowling league. Even sixty years later, I can savor memories of watching from behind as Maureen bowled.

Up until the 50s, bowling alleys were not automated. The new bowling alley didn't spring up in Leesburg until I was in high school; before then we did our bowling in a dingy old building in a suspect part of town. Instead of a machine that set the pins and sent your ball back to you, a kid did the setting and sending. For a while I was that kid.

The bowling alley was one place in town where you could always get a job. Setting pins was awful work, so the turnover rate was high. When I needed extra money, I always knew where I could go. The pay was a whopping dime a game; I'd usually net out fifty cents for an evening's work.

It was a harrowing job that would certainly violate today's workplace standards. It was a flagrant violation of the child labor laws, too, since the average age of pinsetters was probably around eleven years old. It was insanely noisy, with 16-pound balls crashing over and over into the pins a few feet away. You also could get hurt if you didn't keep your wits about you. You perched on a ledge behind the pit the pins crashed into. When the ball hit the pins, you jumped down into the pit to return the ball and put the pins back in the rack. After the second ball, you jumped back into the pit to reset the pins and rack them back into their correct positions. On more than one occasion I didn't get back up on the ledge in time and got my legs bruised by flying pins. Being Florida, it was always hot and sweaty, too.

The boss had a good racket going. When you'd go up to get your dime's pay, he'd ask you if you wanted "pay or pop." He had a chest full of icy cold soda, all of which cost a dime. On an 80-degree Florida evening, flushed and sweaty after setting pins, a frosty bottle of soda looked pretty fetching. Often, I spent half my meager earnings on ice-cold bottles of Pepsi.

Throughout junior high school I was an avid coin collector and trader. I hit upon a great strategy for accumulating valuable coins. In those days just about every kid had a piggy bank, so I simply asked my classmates to bring in their piggy banks for me to inspect. Often, I found valuable coins, and had the pleasure of watching some kid's eyes pop when I handed him a dollar bill for a penny I'd found. On one occasion I found a rare 1909 penny in a kid's piggy bank, gave him two dollars for it, and sold it later that day for $35. My coin trading career came to close in the 9th grade when I discovered girls. I suddenly didn't want to be known as that kid who was always rifling through piles of coins during lunch break. I hung onto some of the most valuable ones, such as my collection of 1927 Standing Liberty quarters, until I sold the whole works in college to finance a spring vacation in Ft. Lauderdale.

I worked as a furniture mover right out of high school, starting at fifty cents an hour at Boyd's Furniture in Leesburg. While the job was brutal and didn't pay much, it gave me a priceless lifetime memory. When I got my first paycheck, for $23, I deposited it over the lunch hour and walked over to Bache & Company, the town's only stockbroker. There, I purchased one share of stock, AVCO Corporation, for $17. The clerk told me I was the only person who'd ever bought just one share of a stock. "Don't worry," I told her, "I'll be back for more."

I had gotten fascinated with the stock market during my senior year of high school, after a neighbor told me about a $10,000 investment that had run up to $100,000 in value when he sold it. That seemed like a modern form of alchemy, another subject I was keen on. With the help of the stockbroker, I had researched AVCO stock carefully, even though I didn't yet have enough money to buy a share. Then came that first paycheck that launched me into the heady world of capitalism, where I'm still an enthusiastic participant. Historical note: I watched my share of AVCO run up to $27 before I sold it, jubilantly pocketing a $10 profit and impressing my girlfriend with a fancy dinner.

Later that summer, Will Grimsley, the father of one of my high school classmates, offered me the astounding sum of a dollar an hour to work as a pump-jockey at his gas station. Young readers may not know that there was a time when you pulled up to a pump and sat in your car while someone filled your tank, cleaned your windshield, checked your oil, and did anything else you wanted, including fetching you a soda out of the machine. Usually, it was elderly ladies who asked me to get them a soda out of the machine. I always got the soda at a sprint, because looking enthusiastic would often earn me a nickel or dime tip.

On one occasion I got an astronomical $1 tip, but I think you'll agree that I earned it. A fellow pulled into the station and asked me if I could give his car's interior a quick cleaning. That service was included in a car wash for $1.50, so I asked him if he wanted the wash, too. "No, just the inside. I'm in a hurry." He pulled it into the bay and got out, leaving the door open. I poked my head in to discover that he had vomited profusely all over the seat and floor. The man said, somewhat sheepishly, "I had a shot of whiskey and I guess my stomach couldn't handle it." He pointed to the ruined interior and said in a glum tone, "There's my breakfast."

I'm going to spare you further details, but it took me fifteen minutes of unpleasant work to clean the interior. I finished by giving it several shots of the so-called "new car" spray we used. The powerful scent smelt like a combination of menthol and bug spray, but it was a great improvement on the whiskey-and-breakfast odor beforehand. Now for the punchline: When I finished, I held out my hand expectantly for the $1.50. "Sorry," the guy said, "I only have a dollar, but hey, you didn't have to do the outside." Resisting the urge to throttle him, I took the dollar and trudged into the office to hand it over to Mr. Grimsley. He listened to my tale and said, "Keep the buck, son."

When I think of my brief career as a pump-jockey, I also remember how hard it was to get windshields clean in Florida, land of all things "bug." Millions of these unfortunate beings come to their untidy end on windshields; I remember times on the night shift when it took me five minutes of hard scrubbing to get all the bug-guts and debris off a windshield. That job also taught me how much I don't like getting my hands dirty. Even though the gas station had a mega-powerful soap to remove grease, I never quite got my hands clean that whole summer. I made a vow then and there never to get another job where I was likely to get my hands dirty.

I came back home after my first year of college and immediately caught a lucky break. My mother, a newspaper reporter and columnist, also did a daily news show on the local radio station. I stopped in to see her do the show one day and fell into conversation with the station manager. He was looking for a weekend DJ, and I talked him into giving me a chance. Two days later, I was sitting in front of the control board talking into a microphone. At first, I did the shifts nobody else wanted, such as 6 a.m. to noon on weekends, but soon I got a weekday show. Four hours on the air five days a week, plus two six-hour weekend shifts gave me a tremendous amount of experience in a short period of time.

On Sunday mornings I ran the controls for radio preachers who rented hours to put their services on the air. One minister, a charismatic elder who called himself Preacher D, came to the station every week to do his show in person. For an hour he would go into a little room separated from me by a glass window and preach a barnburner of a sermon. During the hour he would get progressively more wound up, culminating in a full-out screaming rant of twenty minutes or so. One of Preacher D's major obsessions was the evil cunning of women. Once he did a whole rager of a sermon on how married women "snuck out" and seduced single men then claimed to have been raped if they were caught. I had truly never seen anything like Preacher D. How anyone could get so worked up over such insane subjects mystified me. My last duty at the conclusion of every Preacher D's sermon was to go into the little room and apply Windex to the glass window. In the heights of his passion, Preacher D would dispense a considerable amount of saliva. It wasn't as bad as cleaning bugs off windshields, but it was close.

That summer, I fell in love with radio as a medium, and when I decided to take a break from college after two years, I threw myself wholeheartedly into a radio career. From 1965 to 1968 I worked at the top rock station in Orlando, WLOF, among some of the most creative people I've ever known. There was Pat O'Day in the mornings, me from 10-2, Johnny Gee in drive time, and Bill Vermillion from six to midnight. Our program director was a wildly creative guy named Tom Siegfried, who let us do just about anything we wanted as long as we stayed on top of the ratings.

The '60s were a magical time to be a disc jockey. It was the height of the Beatles era, and my radio station was on the leading edge of it. We premiered a lot of records that would become hits across the country. One of our great coups was to buy a studio bootleg of "A Day in the Life" by the Beatles and become the first station in the U.S. to play that remarkable song on the air. We also co-produced a lot of the biggest concerts. I got to hang out with a whole host of fascinating people, including Jimi Hendrix, future Led Zeppelin star Jimmy Page, Brian Wilson, Bob Seger, the Rascals, the Righteous Brothers, and many others I'm forgetting. I also got into band management and concert promotion for about a year. I handled bookings for a band called Plant Life, which had one modest hit on Columbia's Date Records, "Flower Girl," and lives on into eternity thanks to YouTube.

Younger readers may not know that in the '60s and '70s, DJs on AM radio were much more powerful than they are now, the equivalent of today's Instagram Influencers and YouTube stars. AM radio was the place where you heard the new music. Up until the '70s, few people had radios that could receive FM stations, so AM captured 90% of the ears. For three-plus years I worked at the radio station all day and went to night classes at Rollins to finish up my bachelor's degree. Classes were from 6:30-9:30 p.m., so I'd finish recording commercials at the station at 6, make a mad dash across town just in time to slide into my seat in a Shakespeare class. It took me six years instead of four to get my degree, but I had a VERY good time along the way. Being a young, single guy at the most popular radio station had social benefits beyond my wildest dreams.

After three years, my DJ career ended, thanks to a painful wake-up event. By then I was doing my DJ shift from 10 a.m. to 2 p.m., recording commercials all afternoon, going to college at night, managing a band, and producing rock concerts. Several nights a week I also DJ'd at a strip club from 10 p.m. to 2 a.m. The strippers and I shared the same break room; somewhere there's a photo of me, sitting in the corner eating a sandwich and reading a textbook while a couple of scantily clad young women are having a smoke in the background.

After the club closed, I'd dash back home, with a stop at the Krispy Kreme donut emporium, and collapse into bed by 3 a.m. That is, unless, I was entertaining a guest, which I probably did five nights out of seven. Then, it was up again at 8 a.m. to get ready for my radio shift. Obviously, this was not a sustainable lifestyle, but try to tell that to a 21-year-old who's driving a brand-new Mercedes and walking around with a roll of hundred-dollar bills in his pocket.

In those faraway days, when a new VW Bug cost $1600, a $100 bill was a more compelling piece of paper than it is now. I remember vividly the first time I got paid with one. A concert promoter slapped a hundred into my hand to thank me for talking up his event on the radio. I felt instantly rich and decided on the spot to have at least one in my pocket at all times. Gradually I built up my supply until I was walking around with a big roll, a visible bulge in my right-hand pocket. (Freudian scholars take note.)

Living in the fast lane for three years took its toll, and it all came screeching to a halt one hot Florida afternoon. I'd was hurrying along the sidewalk, wolfing down a Philly cheese-steak sandwich I grabbed to go. I was late to a meeting of the unruly constituents of the band I managed. Suddenly I felt a lightning bolt of pain in my belly—it felt like some-body stuck me in the gut with a pitchfork. It hurt so badly I bent over double, but as fortune would have it, I was stricken right in front of a doctor's office. It was their lunch hour, but the doctor happened to be near the front window. He saw me and unlocked the door so I could come in. He didn't treat me with any pharmaceuticals, but he gave me a different kind of medicine that meant a great deal more. He sat next to me for a while in the waiting room and talked to me. The only thing I can remember from the conversation was he said I needed to look carefully at how I was living my life.

That was about the last thing I wanted to hear. I wanted a slug of something to make my belly stop hurting. He gave me a valuable insight, but at the time I was too busy self-destructing to pay attention.

Although I didn't fully grasp it at the time, I was in a deep depression because of my grandmother's death. One day she was my beloved Granny, always with a smile and a hug when I came to visit. The next day she was on a ventilator after a stroke, with Mom, Aunt Audrey, and me standing beside her laboring body, trying to decide whether to turn off the machine. That moment, that decision, in spite of its obvious necessity, was one of the worst experiences of my life.

Immediately after her death, I went on a binge in practi-cally every way you can imagine, with the exception of alcohol, which thankfully I can only tolerate in tiny amounts. I think I gained fifty pounds in the six months after my grandmother died, in addition to assuaging my grief with a high body-count of overnight visitors. It would take me years before I had enough insight to realize how profoundly the loss of my grandmother affected me in my 20s.

When I finished my bachelor's degree, I didn't know where I wanted to live or what I wanted to do. I just knew I wanted to get out of Florida. My girlfriend of six months, Linda wanted to move back to Maine, where she'd grown up and had family. In retrospect, I would have probably done just about anything to get out of Florida. The solution my unconscious mind came up with was to get into a hasty marriage with a moneyed woman from Maine. Money was high on my mind at the time because I had just gone broke, wiped out financially by a bad night at the box office.

I'd been flying high on the money I'd made producing concerts with the Yardbirds, Rascals and popular regional bands like The Tropics and Plant Life. I felt I could do no wrong, so I doubled down and booked a much larger group, The Hollies, then riding on a string of hits. All was well until the day of the concert when the unthinkable happened: a late hurricane barreled across Central Florida. People stayed away in droves, and I tanked a bundle of money. I had to sell my fancy Mercedes and practically everything else I owned to keep angry creditors off my doorstep.

I piled my meager belongings into Linda's blue Ford Fiesta and made my escape, Linda staying behind to fly up the following week. I never returned, except for brief visits to attend funerals and other family duties.

I have only good things to say about the southern coast of Maine, except for some of the people I met there. Having grown up in the South, I thought I knew something about stubborn fundamentalist racists, but I just hadn't met the New England variety yet. I even enjoyed the unpredictable New England weather, which everybody else seemed to complain about constantly. A beautiful day on the coast of Maine is dazzling, all the more so because there's so few of them. I spent my first twenty-three years in sultry Central Florida, where Tarzan movies were made because of the steamy excellence of the jungles. Maine was the exact opposite, and I found it thrilling to walk along the rocky shoreline on a blustery day, a brisk wind in my face, fantasizing about my life to come as author of the Great American Novel.

My initial plan was to use the summer to write a novel I'd been dreaming up. It was a lofty goal that only lasted a short time. A wiser 23-year-old would probably have known that a) very few 23-year-olds are capable of writing even a Truly Awful American Novel, and b) changing your geography doesn't change your life. It wasn't long before my lack of self-awareness and problems in my relationship caught up with me.

The money supply began to dry up, too, and to make ends meet I got a job in a liquor store. At that time, only state-operated stores were allowed to sell liquor in Maine. Along with my boss, Elwood, and the other clerk, Robert, we serviced the thirsty citizens of southern Maine from our store in Kittery, the first village once you cross the bridge from New Hampshire. There was a New Hampshire liquor store at the other end of the bridge, and because New Hampshire didn't charge sales tax, liquor was much cheaper there. The citizens of southern Maine were all too willing to flaunt the law to get their libations. They could cross the bridge into New Hampshire and buy a $10 bottle of wine for $7. As a result, we got almost no walk-in customers.

Maine restaurants were required to buy from us, though, so our business, such as it was, consisted of several half-hour flurries of work during the day getting orders ready for restaurant pickups. The rest of the time there was nothing to do. It was a dream job for a writer. On the average, I probably spent four hours of my day sitting in the dim back room of the store at a little metal desk, scribbling away with my Bic pen and yellow legal pad. I'd like to take this opportunity to send belated thanks to the Maine Liquor Commission for giving me a couple of months of relative leisure to hone my craft.

The job was only temporary for the summer, so as September approached, I began scanning the newspaper ads to find a "real" job. I applied for a job as a copywriter at an ad agency, but before I got to the interview, I saw something better. "English teacher needed immediately, private school." Private school meant that a state teaching credential wasn't necessary. The school was only a half hour or so away, in the tiny town of Center Strafford, New Hampshire, so I called and was invited to come that evening for an interview. They told me a teacher had suddenly quit only ten days before school started.

When I went for my interview, I discovered a few important facts that had been left out of the advertisement. The facts revealed at the interview had the qualities of a Good News/ Bad News joke. Bad News: this wasn't the type of private school I'd pictured, with earnest young scholars from patrician families and me puffing thoughtfully on a pipe, clad in a corduroy blazer with elbow patches. This was a private school where delinquent teenage boys were sent to get straightened out. There were about a hundred of them housed in three dormitories. Good News: the job came with a free two-bedroom apartment. Bad News: the free apartment was connected to one of the dormitories, and I would be in charge of its 24 residents all day and all night.

I contemplated this new reality: I would be living in a 500-square-foot apartment with a wife I didn't want to be married to, our new baby, and a couple dozen juvenile delinquents. In retrospect, I probably should have bolted from the interview and run screaming to the ad agency. But, no, all I could think about was a free apartment and the long summer off. Like many private schools, this one started late and ended early. For a budding writer, the idea of having May 15 - September 1 to practice my craft was practically a dream come true.

I was offered the job, for the grand sum of $110 a week. "Sounds great," I said. "When can we move in?"

I've written in other books about my adventures at the school, so let me just hit a few high spots. My first day of teaching, which I shall never forget, I came home after work with a blinding headache aspirin couldn't touch. I wasn't used to being stared at all day with a range of gazes that communicated sullen hostility, dumbfounded incomprehension, and thinly concealed contempt. These were tough kids from tough backgrounds, and I had never spent a day of my life around juvenile delinquents. I had a lot of learning to do.

One stroke of good fortune was becoming friends with Neil Marinello, the school counselor, who turned me on to the University of New Hampshire counseling program. I don't think I could have survived the two years at the school if I hadn't gotten the training from the UNH program, which thankfully was only twenty minutes away. The teaching part of my day was the easy part. After school let out, I had to be available for handling whatever dormitory dramas took place, ranging from squabbles to full-out brawls and runaways. It was hard work, far from the corduroy blazer life I'd envisioned.

After two years at the school, and armed with my new master's degree in counseling, I got a job as the clinical director of a halfway house for delinquents in Manchester, New Hampshire. The salary was great, nearly three times what I was making as a teacher, but I soon discovered I was terrible at the job. The clinical work with the boys was okay, but I turned out to be woefully unskilled at the administrative part of the job. I got fired after six months, and although it stung me at the time, it turned out to be one of the best things that ever happened to me. It inspired me to apply to the Stanford Ph.D. program in counseling psychology. By then I'd fallen so in love with the field of counseling psychology that I couldn't imagine ever doing anything else.

The great thing about the Stanford program was the deep immersion it gave me in working with a wide variety of clients. As part of my training, I saw clients at the Stanford Institute for Behavioral Counseling. Each week would begin with case assignment, where a stack of file folders would be handed out to a half dozen of us interns. Opening each folder was to me like opening a present. I never knew if the person inside the folder was going to be a teacher with anxiety disorder, a runaway teenager, a lonely widower, a high-tech executive, or a couple with sexual dysfunction in their relationship. I worked with all those and dozens more clients during the two-plus years I worked there. It was the best kind of training, where every day I got to find out how counseling theories worked in real life. I will always be grateful for the wealth of practical knowledge I got at Stanford.

As soon as I got my Ph.D. I began seeing private clients while at the same time working as a research psychologist at Stanford. Partway through that year, I got wind of an assistant professor job that had opened up at the Colorado Springs branch of University of Colorado. I went out to interview for the job and fell in love with Colorado the moment I stepped off the plane. After breathing the sullied air of the Bay Area for several years, my first breath of Colorado air was so delicious I can remember it to this day. The wide, open spaces and stunning beauty of the mountains also made a big impact on me. I got the job, and in August of 1974 I packed all my belongings into my VW Bug and drove to Colorado. I ended up staying there two decades, rising through the ranks eventually to become chairman of the Counseling Psychology department.

Being a university professor had great satisfactions to it, but I found some aspects of the job very frustrating. I loved teaching my classes and working with the graduate students in their internships. I didn't mind the "publish or perish" mentality that irked a lot of the professors, because I'd written numerous journal articles and published several books. What drove me batty were the endless committee meetings about matters of minimal relevance. The glacial pace of the meetings was especially frustrating. Every tiny issue had to be discussed from every possible angle, with committees and sub-committees assigned to mull over the various facets.

My first campus-wide faculty meeting lives vividly in my memory. The dean proposed a new idea: changing to plus-and-minus grading instead of just A,B,C, D and F. Just the mention of it set off a storm of passionate arguments in the room. After listening to people spout their opinions for a half hour, I grew frustrated and stuck up my hand. The dean called on me and I introduced myself as the new assistant professor in the counseling department. "Here's a simple solution," I said. "How about if we try it out for a year and see if we like it?"

To my surprise, my suggestion was greeted by a wave of derisive laughter. From their reaction, one might have thought I'd proposed a Nude Faculty Calendar. One of my colleagues saw my confusion and leaned over to explain it to me. They were laughing at my naivete' for suggesting something so preposterous as "trying it out." Things weren't done that way. Instead, the dean assigned a special committee to study the issue, asking them to give a progress report on their deliberations each month. That process continued for the next decade and spawned several sub-committees. Roll the clock forward twelve years for the punchline to my story: after more than a hundred committee meetings, the faculty voted to try it for a year!

Almost as soon as Katie and I got together in 1980, we started offering seminars on breathwork, movement therapy, and the new transformational ideas we were generating. With Katie's private practice, our seminars and my university work, we kept quite busy throughout the '80s.

In 1995, after 21 years at the university, I took early retirement and we moved to Santa Barbara, Katie's hometown. Her parents were getting up in years, so we bought a house in nearby Montecito so we could look after them. We set up our institute in a building that had once been the superior courthouse in Santa Barbara.

Around that same time, I also got involved in the movie business, leading to a plethora of new jobs as a screenwriter, producer, and, in a one-time-only performance, as an actor. I stress "one-time-only" because I've never had the urge to get on that side of the camera again. In my key scene, we ended up doing eleven takes over a three-hour period. The professional actors in the scene didn't mind doing one take after another, because it gave them opportunities to fine-tune their performance. By contrast, I was virtually homicidal by the time we got to the last take.

I've been on hundreds of television shows without a moment of nervousness that I can remember. Acting was different; it froze my innards tight. On television shows I am usually talking about one of my books or commenting on something as an expert. I'm being myself, so there's nothing to get nervous about. Pretending to be someone else, though, was one of the most nervous-making things I've ever done. Having to produce emotion on demand turned out to be impossible for me, probably because I've gone to great lengths in my life to discover and bring to light my authentic emotions. (Scholars of Hendricks trivia can find my performance living on into eternity via YouTube. Do a search for the short film, *Five Wishes*.)

Between book projects one summer, I wrote an original script for a quirky cop movie, a genre I always enjoy. The script caught the eye of a producer/director who optioned it right away. In true Hollywood fashion, the movie never got made, but through it I made a lifechanging connection at a party at the director's house in Brentwood. A producer named Stephen Simon was at the party, bringing with him the trailer for his movie that was about to open, *What Dreams May Come*. The trailer was breathtaking in its visuals, which later won an Oscar, and for Robin Williams' sensitive portrayal of the bereaved husband. Stephen and I struck up a friendship that led to many adventures in trying to get inspirational movies produced by a movie industry that wasn't interested.

One morning in late 2003, I had the flash of an idea just after meditation. "Hmm, since we're not having any success pitching inspirational movies to Hollywood studios, let's just hot-wire around Hollywood. We'll find inspiring movies at film festivals and send them directly to people on DVD." That ten-second flash of an idea would eventually make millions of dollars for us and the investors. With Stephen as the spokesperson and me in the background as CEO, we launched Spiritual Cinema Circle in 2004 and were thrilled to watch it grow within a few years to serve 25,000 members in 80 different countries.

I love creating an enterprise and getting it to profitability, but the actual running of a business is not fun at all for me. As soon as possible, I handed off the reins of Spiritual Cinema Circle to a "real" businessperson, a Harvard MBA who pulled the levers much better than I ever could. I served as board chairman and took on special projects, such as being executive producer on the feature film we made of *Conversations with God*. Eventually the operation got so big that I sold it to a large company in 2008. I launched the business with $100,000 of my own money and sold it for a multimillion-dollar payout, a satisfying bit of financial alchemy. I did the same thing with another business, Illumination University, a collection of e-courses on self-esteem, relationships, and health. It took me a year to create it and get it running, but as soon as it had money in the bank, I sold it to another company to run.

When I was in my thirties, I made a crucial decision to create a job I'd never want to retire from. That decision turned out far better than I could ever have imagined. Four decades later, that dream is still coming true every day. I wake up every morning excited about the creative projects I'm working on, the courses I teach, and the people I mentor. Now, since the advent of FaceTime, Zoom, and Skype, I'm able to spend quality time with people I care about all over the world.

CHAPTER TEN

PEDALING TO LHASA, SOBBING TO TASHILUMPO

I've been fascinated by Tibet since I was eight or nine years old. I remember my mother taking me to the Leesburg Public Library and the librarian recommending the Hardy Boys mysteries. I was immediately hooked. Fortunately, there were dozens of the books, so I was able to stay happily enthralled by their adventures for several years. The one that made the biggest impression on me was about Frank and Joe's adventure in Tibet. Mysterious monasteries, robed monks, incense, fireworks ....it all fired up my already-overheated imagination. Soon, I was pretending in neighborhood games to be a Tibetan lama. I remember playing the role of the "mysterious lama who came to town" in a couple of Old West dramas we staged. In the fifth grade I got a globe for my birthday, and the first thing I asked my brother to show me was where Tibet was located.

As a grownup, I continued to read everything I could get my hands on about Tibet, from coffee-table photograph books to the impenetrable tomes on Tibetan Buddhism by Herbert Guenther. I wanted to go there so badly I could practically taste the yak butter. I couldn't get near Tibet, though, because in those days Tibet was sealed off by the Chinese invaders who stormed the country in 1959. Gradually, the

Chinese began to let in visitors, mostly by way of expensive guided tours, but that approach to Tibet didn't interest me in the least.

By the mid-80s, I had become an avid mountain-biker. I lived in the foothills of the Rockies in those days, prime biking territory, and almost every good-weather day found me astride my tricked-out Klein mountain bike, chugging up a trail or screaming down one. One day, I was leafing through a bicycling magazine when a small ad caught my attention. Twelve visas had been issued for mountain bike travel in Tibet! The visas were for three weeks in August of 1986. First come, first served! My application and check were in the mail within the hour. A month later, I was notified that I was among the chosen. Katie wasn't interested in going; not only is she unenthusiastic about rough travel, but we had also just moved into our new home in Colorado, a 100-year-old Victorian that needed her attention.

In August, the twelve of us met up in San Francisco and boarded a plane operated by the mainland Chinese government. None of us knew each other beforehand, but we quickly bonded on the trip over, partly because I think we were only people out of the 300 on the plane who weren't puffing on cigarettes. I don't think I've ever been quite as miserable for so many hours as I was on that plane. The cigarette smoke was so thick in the cabin that it looked like the swirling mists in classic Chinese paintings. Fortunately, we'd been advised to bring surgical masks to protect against the high air pollution in Beijing, where we'd be spending the first few days. With a surgical mask and a scarf wrapped around my face I got enough air to stay alive, but that's about all. When we got off the plane in Beijing, even the awful air of that city was a welcome relief.

There were various adventures in and around Beijing before we set off for Chengdu, the nearest Chinese city to Tibet. One costly "adventure" was that the State Police, one of the most corrupt organizations on earth, paid us a visit and told us we hadn't paid some obscure tax on "the importation of foreign-made bicycles." They wanted $800, which seemed outlandishly high even if it had been legal. We argued that yes, we were importing the bikes, but we were going to export them in a few weeks. Oops. Now they wanted $1600! It was a shakedown, pure and simple, and when we refused to be shook down, they took all our bikes and impounded them. Finally, after a couple of days of intense negotiations, a suitably smaller bribe was agreed upon and our bikes reappeared, none the worse for wear.

My entry into Tibet wasn't quite the glorious moment I'd been anticipating. Almost as soon as I stepped off the plane I got hit by a blinding headache. I had done some training before I left home, but I found on my first day in Tibet that no amount of training can prepare you for riding a bike at 12,000-14,000 feet of altitude. The headache hung around for three days, no matter how many aspirin I took.

In spite of various physical discomforts, being in Tibet felt like pure magic to me. I got to wander through all the places that had lived in my imagination for so long. I explored the labyrinths of the Potala, with its thousand chapels (according to legend—I didn't actually count them) and its musty smell of yak-butter candles permeating the atmosphere. I prostrated myself with thousands of other Buddhist pilgrims on the Barkhor, the holy path around the city. Finally, after a week of journeys around Lhasa, including visiting the ancient Drepung and Sera monasteries, we set off on what for me would be the truly life-changing part of the trip.

Floods had wiped out some of the road between Lhasa and Shigatse, the second-largest city in Tibet and home of the Tashilumpo monastery. We ended up putting the bikes on the back of a big truck which dropped us off at the top of a 17,000-foot pass about fifty miles from Tashilumpo. After an hour of getting organized at the top of the pass (and feeling stoned on the thin air at that height), we mounted up and set off toward our destination of the Tashilumpo monastery. The first hour of the journey was one of the most exhilarating rides of my life—downhill all the way to 12,000 feet on a twisting gravel road. A twisting road without a single barrier between us and a thousand-foot drop-off! It made for an unparalleled clarity of focus. Fortunately, we all got to the flatland intact, and paused briefly to celebrate at the side of one of the most beautiful lakes I've ever seen.

The second hour of the journey was a different story. We rode up and down dozens of hills, plus pedaling twenty-some miles into a stiff wind. The physical challenge was more intense than anything I'd ever experienced. I was around forty years old at the time, and in pretty good shape for a person of my age. That ride, though, pushed me to my edge. A couple of the riders were hardy twenty-somethings who outdistanced the rest of us by miles. The rest of us spread out pretty much according to age, with our sixty-somethings bringing up the rear a couple of miles behind. As the wind blew harder, my determination to get to Tashilumpo only got stronger. Soon I was pedaling in first gear at about two miles per hour, at the very limit of my body's strength.

At one point my physical exhaustion got to the point that I started hallucinating about my grandmother. She had been dead for twenty years, but I somehow got the impression that if I got to Tashilumpo I could see her again. My exertion became frantic in my push to hurry up so I could get there quicker. Eventually, though, I saw through the fantasy. It didn't have anything to do with getting to Tashilumpo. It was really about opening up to my love for my grandmother and my grief about her absence from my life. I stood up on the pedals in the howling wind and opened my heart to the sadness I felt. I was gasping massive gulps of air in and out as I pedaled along, sobbing uncontrollably about my grandmother's love that I would never feel again. Even now as I write this, I feel the sweet power of her love deep inside me and the ache of missing her physical presence. I would give anything to hear her voice one more time or feel the strength of her hand touching mine.

At the peak of my straining, just when I thought I couldn't go any further without collapsing, I felt the blossoming of a new awareness inside me: the realization that at the deepest level of myself I AM my grandmother's love. There was no way I could lose her love, not ever—it was in every cell of my being. My grandmother's love lived in me and I lived in it. It couldn't go anywhere—it was there for all time.

Then, a seeming miracle happened in the outside world. I pedaled around a curve and caught the wind, which had been in my face for the past hour, suddenly at my back. Now I was flying along at twenty miles an hour rather than creeping along at two. My breath was still rushing powerfully in and out of my lungs, but now it came and went freely in the huge open space that had been cleared of my ancient grief. I flew down the road, celebrating with big lungfuls of pristine pure air. In the distance, I saw small dwellings signaling the outskirts of Shigatse. I came into town standing up on my pedals, waving at monks and kids who waved back with big smiles on their faces.

I found my way through the back streets, guided by kids pointing the direction, and braked to a stop at the gate of Tashilumpo Monastery. I paused to say a prayer of gratitude before I went in. I gave thanks for my grandmother and for the elegant workings of fate that had brought me to that place. A gong sounded, and from within the monastery I heard the low drone of monks chanting. I went through the gate, along with my rainbow of Lycra-clad colleagues, where we were welcomed by smiling monks coming forward to place white scarves around our necks. Just like in the Hardy Boys book.

CHAPTER ELEVEN

THROWN OFF THE BUS
AT THE BORDER

I'll never forget the night my bus got busted on the India-Nepal border.

In 1980, I spent a month trekking around India and Nepal, complete with backpack, long hair, and granny-glasses. I stayed at ashrams, met lots of gurus, hiked the Himalayan backcountry, and spent many happy hours in cafés sipping chai and savoring the remarkable hashish available in that part of the world.

One way I got from place to place was on top of buses. It was April and so hot that often the only tolerable way to ride was up on top, surrounded by piles of duffel bags and suitcases. It was still hot, but at least you had the breeze from the moving bus instead of being packed in with forty or fifty sweltering passengers. I had many wonderful conversations with fellow travelers on bus tops, including one I'll always be grateful for. A Danish guy swapped his battered copy of *One Hundred Years of Solitude* to me for the book I'd just finished, *Watership Down*. Those two books are among my life's greatest reading experiences. If you haven't read these two master-works, go get them now—they'll change your life.

The most memorable of all my bus journeys was my final one, when I was trying to cross the border from Nepal back into India. My plane ticket back to London left from New Delhi. I had a leisurely three days to get to Delhi, so I opted to save money by going via bus. I paid $10 for the ticket, and we left Katmandu in late morning on a renovated school bus. After a long and bumpy day on the road, we lumbered up to the border crossing with India after dark.

There, things went awry.

Our bus was in a long line of vehicles, so it took us almost an hour to creep forward to where officials were checking papers. The bus driver, who was also the entrepreneur who had organized the bus trip, got into a loud argument with the officials over his paperwork. After a half hour of shouting back and forth, the officials solved the problem by literally dragging the driver off the bus. Soldiers clambered aboard and herded all of us passengers off at gunpoint. They threw our bags off the top and marched off, leaving us to fend for ourselves. For the next couple of hours, we milled around, getting our visas stamped and trying to find out when the bus would be released.

Then it got even crazier. The bus driver emerged from the officials' office, looking very bedraggled, and got us together on the tarmac. He told us the bus had been seized, but he would lead us to a nearby town that had a railroad station. By this time, it was getting on toward midnight and some of us were falling asleep on our feet. Nevertheless, we set off on foot down the road with the bus driver leading the way. After a while we turned on to a smaller road that was completely unlit and had thick jungle on either side of the narrow track.

I was walking just behind the bus driver when there was an audible rustling in the bushes beside the road. The driver froze. I asked him what was wrong, and he said the sound had scared him. I asked him what he was afraid of,. "Tigers," he hissed. "Lots of tigers around here."

Until that moment, I don't believe I'd ever considered having to deal with an actual tiger.

Our driver/leader had been there before, though, and had a solution of sorts. He herded us all together and had us walk down the road in a tightly clustered clump. Picture a bunch of American, German, and other Western hippies jammed together with a dozen others, including Nepalese, Indians, and one Muslim fellow with two veiled wives, each carrying a baby. Needless to say, our journey down the road was slow and jerky. At one point, our procession came to a halt while the Muslim guy peeled an orange and divided it equally between his wives.

We bumbled our way along the trail, fortunately free of tigers, until we got to a train stop. There I parted company with my fellow travelers and climbed aboard a decrepit train to Delhi. Although it was night-time, it was still brutally hot inside the train. I found an empty seat, collapsed on it, and promptly sank into exhausted sleep.

An hour later, I was jostled awake to the squealing of brakes and the train grinding to a stop. We seemed to be in the middle of nowhere, and my first thought was something like "Oh, no, here we go again." It turned out that we had simply stopped for fuel, but the pause enabled all sorts of hawkers to come aboard with tea, fruit, and other comestibles. I bought a couple of bananas and was munching on one when a man with a broom lurched up to my seat. His face was flushed and he was breathing alcohol fumes. I saw red spittle dripping off his chin and realized he was also high on betel nut.

He shouted something unintelligible to me and stirred the dust around my seat with his broom. I couldn't figure out what he was shouting at me about, so I summoned the conductor to translate. The conductor spoke such heavily accented English that I had a hard time understanding him, too. After a few frustrating back-and-forth's I realized he was saying, "This is train sweeper. You must tip him."

Still bleary from exhaustion and irritated that I'd been jolted out of my nap, I pointed at the filthy floor and said, "I'm supposed to tip him for that?" This sent the sweeper into a tirade at me, fortunately completely unintelligible. He also started sweeping furiously around my seat, raising a cloud of dust that caused me to start sneezing. Finally, I gave the guy a couple of rupees to make him stop his mad assault on the dirty floor. He departed with a victorious smirk, which I had no trouble translating as "See? You should have tipped me the first time I asked."

We're about to have a happy ending to the story, but first I should mention that when I got on the bus in Katmandu, I'd been hiking in the Himalayas for two weeks and looked it. I was shaggy of hair and whisker; my battered jeans and tee-shirt were forlorn and nearing the end of their lifespans. Other than a couple of cold showers, it had been a week or so since I'd had a bath.

I'd dropped about fifteen pounds in two weeks of hiking. I'd been living on rice and lentils, the ubiquitous and often only dish on the trekking routes through the Himalayas. When I finally stumbled off the train in Delhi, I was tired, hungrier than I'd ever been in my life, and looked much the worse for wear. I found a nearby hotel, Claridge's, and splurged $30 for a room. There, I sank happily into a hot bath and ordered up a magnificent room-service meal. According to my notebook, I had two types of curry, tandoori chicken, and rice biryani. For dessert, I had warm carrot pudding and kulfi, the Indian ice cream, spiced with cardamom.

After a twelve-hour sleep, I went down to get a haircut and a shave in the hotel salon. Thanks to the exemplary sales skills of the staff, I also ended up getting a neck massage as well as the very first facial and manicure of my life. The whole works cost $5 including a tip, and I walked out of the salon looking, literally, like a different person. When I went to the front desk to get some change, even the clerk who'd checked me in the night before didn't recognize me.

CHAPTER TWELVE

BASEBALL AND ME

I've loved baseball for as long as I can remember. That love was strengthened by the good bit of my childhood I spent in the baseball park my granddad managed.

Here's how it went all summer long, from the time I was about seven to when I entered my teens. Granddad and I slept in a screened-in room attached to the back of the house. In Southern terms it's called a "sleeping porch." Granddad would wake me up at six a.m. and we'd troop in for the breakfast my grandmother always cooked. My granddad had the same breakfast every day for as long as I knew him: two fried eggs, two strips of bacon, two pieces of buttered toast, and coffee lightened with canned evaporated milk. I never saw him eat a vegetable other than potatoes. I heard he'd tried broccoli early in his life and it had put him off vegetables for all time. He also loved beer, smoked cigars all day, chewed tobacco, and lived to 93.

Granddad and I would set off for the baseball park after breakfast, either on foot or, if my grandmother was in the mood, riding in their ancient Chevrolet. As I mentioned earlier, Granddad didn't drive, so it was up to my grandmother's whims as to whether she'd give us a ride. If she was angry at Granddad about something, which she often was, we'd go to the ballpark on "shanks' mare," my grandfather's phrase for foot travel.

Leesburg had a minor league team that played in the Florida State League, along with Tampa, Daytona, and other towns around central Florida. For part of my childhood, it was a minor league affiliate of the Philadelphia Phillies, then later the Baltimore Orioles. I don't remember much about the Phillies years, but I have many vivid memories of the Orioles years. The team was managed by Cal Ripken, Sr., father of the future legend, Cal Ripken, Jr. I remember seeing Cal, Jr. and his brother, Billy, when they were preschoolers, hanging out at the park with their dad before games.

For a baseball nut, Central Florida was an ideal place to live. In those days, almost all the major league teams came down to Florida for spring training. For the whole month of March every year, it was possible to see the greatest baseball players up close in the small ballparks of Daytona, Tampa, Vero Beach, and other spring training cities. I still remember the thrill of seeing amazing players like Pete Rose and Tim McCarver when they were 20-year-olds, knowing they were on their way to being superstars.

Granddad was an athlete in his youth. He'd grown up near St. Louis in the same generation as great early baseball stars such as Honus Wagner, Ty Cobb, and Christy Mathewson, Grandad's favorite pitcher of all time. He would have loved nothing more to be a professional ballplayer himself, but he wasn't blessed with good vision. As he put it, "Curveballs mystified me." He also was missing part of his left ring finger, due to an accident when he was a young man.

As Granddad's assistant, I learned how to do everything from laying out the chalk baselines to running the scoreboard lights. I raked the clay of the infield hundreds of times, and when it rained, which it often did in Florida, I was on the crew that rushed out onto the field to roll out the canvas tarps. My grandfather spotted early in my life that I loved learning new things, so he kept me busy with any number of activities. The best part, of course, was getting to hang around the ballplayers and see all the games.

As far as my own baseball skills, there were none. It was bitterly disappointing to me that I wasn't any good at hitting, running, pitching, or fielding, those being the key requirements for a baseball player. Granddad was probably just as disappointed; according to the family story, he started playing catch with me almost as soon as I could stand upright. In fact, I remember him spending hours training me to be right-handed, even though I was a natural left-hander, so I could play more positions in my baseball career. When I was a teenager, he got to see me play on the football team, where I was a defensive tackle. I still didn't have any athletic skill at the time, but I was big and took up a lot of space on the line.

Although I played football and was a shot-putter on the track team, baseball was always my first love. Since I didn't have the ability to play on a team, I put my attention on strategy and statistics. I grilled Granddad on the technicalities of when to call for a bunt, how to execute a suicide steal, and other intricacies of the game. I also became a walking repository of baseball statistics. Granddad would ask me something like "Do you happen to remember how many times Babe Ruth struck out in '27, that year he hit 60 homers?"

"Sure, Granddad. 89."

"That's my boy."

Granddad also sneaked in lots of life wisdom into our conversations, some of which was useful and some decidedly not. For example, my grandmother asked him to have The Talk with me about sex. Later, on a walk back from the ballpark, he dispensed the following wisdom, which was the sum total of everything he ever said about sex to me.

"Let me tell you a story, feller. (That was one of Granddad's nicknames for me.) There was once a little dog trotting along and saw a long train coming down the tracks. The little dog wanted to cross the track before the train got there. He ran like crazy and almost made it but the train roared past and cut off the tip of his tail. It was just a small piece, and he could have done fine without it, but he ran back to try to retrieve it. When he tried to get the piece, he slipped, and the train cut off his head. You know what the moral of that story is, feller?"

"Uh, no, Granddad."

"The moral is: don't lose your head over a little piece of tail."

That was it, the only sex education I ever got from a member of the older generation.

I'm afraid it didn't stick, either.

In his spare time, Granddad was a teacher in the local Masonic Lodge. Often in the evenings, he would sit out on the front porch in his rocking chair, smoking cigars and teaching young Masons who were preparing for tests. When I would ask him what they talked about, he'd always just say, "God."

Although he never gave me any specific spiritual instructions, Granddad often played mind-games with me. "Do you know how to catch a bird?" he asked me one day. I was probably seven years old at the time.

"No, Granddad, how?"

"Sneak up to it and put salt on its tail."

I remember being mystified the first time he told me that and was still mystified a few days later when he asked me again if I knew how to catch a bird.

"Put salt on its tail?" I said.

"Yep."

I remember him asking me that question several times over a couple of weeks. Finally, one day I got it. I said, "Granddad, if you're going to the trouble of putting salt on the bird's tail, why not just grab the bird?"

The twinkle in his eye told me he'd just been waiting for me to see the absurdity of catching a bird by putting salt on its tail. Granddad chuckled and said, "That's my boy."

As a grown-up I've changed my team loyalties several times, even though in my deepest heart of hearts, I will always be a Brooklyn Dodgers fan. To me, these scrappy, perpetual underdogs were the perfect baseball team. Even now, sixty-some years later, just saying their names gives me a thrill: Sandy Koufax, Duke Snider, Gil Hodges, Pee Wee Reese, Don Newcombe. The 1955 World Series, when the Dodgers beat the Yankees in the 7th game, was the absolute epiphany of my young baseball life. It was all the sweeter because I was the lone Dodger fanatic in a neighborhood full of kids who loved the loathsome Yankees. Even though I loved Mickey Mantle, I hated the Yankees, who were always stacking the deck with expensive talent their big-city money could buy.

When I was in graduate school at Stanford, I went to my first Giants game at Candlestick Park. Despite the wind currents and frigid temperatures, I became a Giants fan. This phase lasted until the early 90s, when the Colorado Rockies opened their franchise. Katie and I had great seats on the first base line, seven rows up. Our seats were just in front of former Senator Gary Hart, leading to many interesting conversations during games. We moved back to California in 1995 but I remained a Rockies fan for ten years or so after I left Colorado. Now, my allegiance is to the Dodgers again.

I'm writing this just before spring training in 2021. Coming out of the pandemic year of 2020, I'm especially looking forward to the new season, when attending a game in Dodger Stadium might be possible. I've missed the joys of attending 'live' games, the sounds of the crowd, and of course, the traditional chomping of a Dodger Dog. Frankly (pun intended), I don't ever eat hot dogs anywhere else. When I'm in the ballpark, though, certain traditions must be maintained: peanuts, hot dogs, beer. Katie and I bring our own organic roasted-in-the-shell peanuts, but the seventh-inning stretch will find me standing in line for a Dodger Dog and a beer.

In the minor league park I grew up in, a hot dog was a quarter, a Coke was a dime, and they didn't sell beer. Now, a hot dog and a beer at Dodger Stadium will cost you more than twenty bucks. Ticket prices are exorbitant, too, but before you even get up to the window you've already spent $25 to park your car. One of my tech guys took his wife and three kids to a game at the end of last season and came home moaning that the whole works had cost him almost $200. For that reason, going to a major league game is out of reach for many people. I feel sad about that.

I also think the insanely high players' salaries cast a different feeling over the game. As a kid, I remember the buzz in my neighborhood when Mickey Mantle got a $100,000 yearly contract. Now, a big hitter makes $10,000 every time he strolls up to the plate, whether he strikes out or hits a homer. Baseball fans can't help but wonder if all the money that's come into the game has taken something out of it.

Like a lot of old-time fans, I've looked with disfavor on some of the changes in the game. I found it painful to witness the steroid era, seeing players like Barry Bonds and Mark McGwire inflate their arms to Popeye-size dimensions and blow past home run records set by drug-free heroes of mine such as Hank Aaron. I've also been through a few eras when the baseball authorities juiced up the ball (making it springier so players hit more homeruns) to lure more fans into the parks. Then, there's the DH, the designated hitter, about which I have divided feelings. Traditionalists like me say that pitchers have had to go up to bat from the beginnings of baseball. The fact that most of them can't hit brings a wild, random factor to the game. However, I can also see why a manager wouldn't want to expose a $30 million pitcher to the vagaries of the plate, especially when one of those vagaries is the 100-mph fastball of the opposing pitcher.

In spite of all the changes, I still love baseball and hope to be checking those box scores the rest of my life. As long as there's the crack of a bat and the sound of an exuberant baseball crowd, I'll be there. As long as hot dogs are sold in the ballparks of the world, you'll find me with one in hand in the middle of the seventh inning, smacking my lips as I squirt a yellow stripe of mustard down its glistening length. As a kid, I loaded up my dog with mustard, ketchup, mayo, onions, and that Day-Glo green relish they had back then. In my adult life I've become a mustard-only minimalist. Any way you like it, though, I think every baseball fan can agree that no hot dog tastes better than one you eat in a ballpark.

Not long ago I had the pleasure of standing in line at the concession stand behind a father and son, both of them excited to get their Dodger Dogs. From their conversation I learned that it was the little guy's first one. He carried it over to the condiments table, where I was putting mustard on mine, and proceeded to load his hot dog up to the max. Out of the corner of my eye I watched as he took a huge bite and chomped it, his face the very picture of bliss. I knew exactly how he felt.

CHAPTER THIRTEEN

CELEBRATING MY DAUGHTER, AMANDA HENDRICKS

This is a note of appreciation for Amanda, my only child, now an artist living her creative dreams aboard on a houseboat in the Bay Area. In addition to loving her for the past fifty-some years, I've also enjoyed her lively wit, her courage to pursue her artistic dreams, and her ability to survive and thrive through life's challenges.

Like me, Amanda is a Floridian by birth, first coming out into the light in the wee hours of a September morning in 1967. The next year, we moved up to New England, where her mother, Linda, was from. More than fifty years later, that first summer in New England still feels magical to me. The weather was often glorious that summer, the first one I'd ever spent outside muggy Florida. I'd never been anywhere that wasn't humid pretty much all the time; In Maine that summer, I felt a sense of liberation from the bondage of sticky air.

On those glorious days I'd bundle Amanda into a backpack and we'd walk miles on the trail that winds along the rocky seashore. Taking walks in nature became a tradition for us. I have many happy memories of hiking with her in her younger years.

There happened to be a lobster glut that summer; I could walk down to the dock and buy a couple of good-sized crustaceans right off the boat for a buck a piece. These were lobsters like nothing I'd ever tasted: rich, tender meat that was completely different from the spiny, clawless lobsters common to Florida and the Caribbean. I remember Amanda trying a little bite of lobster when she was just learning to eat solid food. She lit up with delight, and later in life it became a favorite food of hers.

Amanda took her first steps in New Hampshire, where we were blessed to live out in the countryside. Once she got her legs under, every nice day would find us out exploring the paths and byways of the area. A comment she made on one of those walks became a family story and is also a good insight into her personality. She was about four years old at the time. We had trudged slowly, with many stops along the way, to the top of a big hill. Resting at the summit, Amanda announced that she had just climbed her first mountain. Then she turned philosophical.

"Daddy, do you know the best way to climb a mountain?"

"No, how?"

"One step at a time."

Amanda's middle name, Delle, comes from my beloved grandmother, Rebecca Dell. I can't remember why we spelled Amanda's middle name with an 'e' on the end of Dell. My grandmother passed away two years before Amanda was born, and one of my life's regrets is that Amanda never got to meet her great-grandmother. I think they would have adored each other.

Due to geography, Amanda never got to know my mother, her "Florida" grandmother very well, either. Because we lived in New England and later California (and because I was chronically short of money in Amanda's younger years,) Amanda only got to visit Florida on rare occasions. Also, my mother was a staunch non-flyer, which also limited Amanda's contact with her. Mom loved being a grandparent to my brother's three children; I regret that she was not able to participate more in Amanda's life.

Amanda's other grandmother, Eleanor Fry, was a chilly New Englander who was reasonably pleasant until she got a couple of drinks in her. On our visits I got used to whisking Amanda off for a long walk when her grandmother and Linda would get into one of their alcohol-fueled screaming matches. (To her great credit, Linda discovered the power of 12-Step work a few years later and changed her life.)

The one thing above all that you need to know about Amanda Hendricks: she's been an artist since she could hold a hold a pencil in her hand. As a child she could spend hours cutting out and arranging bits of colored paper into collages. I noticed at an early age her intensity of focus when she was creating something artistic.

Here's a bit of dialogue that happened more than once:

Dad: Amanda, time to come eat. Dinner's ready.
(No response from Amanda, in her room working on an
    art project.)
Dad: AMANDA! IT'S DINNER TIME!
(Dead silence.)
(Dad marches to door of Amanda's room and looks in.
    Amanda is sitting on the floor, surrounded by materi-
    als, working diligently on a project.)
Dad: DIDN'T YOU HEAR ME?
(Amanda looks up with blank stare.)
Amanda: Sorry, what?

Later, when she was about nine years old, Amanda announced to me that she didn't intend to get married until she was "old." I asked her what age she considered old and she promptly said, "27." I was past 30 at the time, so I was a bit chagrined to be beyond "old" in her mind. Nevertheless, I pressed forward and asked her why she wasn't going to get married until she got to the ancient age of 27. She'd obviously thought it through, because she had her answer at the ready. She said, "Because it would interfere with my art work."

She made good on that commitment, too. She's still an artist and still hasn't married. She lives on a boat in Marin County, and I bet if we dropped in on her today, we'd find her on the deck or in the cabin, surrounded by art materials.

In the spirit of transparency, I should tell you that I only visit the boat virtually, via FaceTime. I have a history of getting dreadfully seasick on boats, whether it's a 75-foot yacht or a ten-foot rowboat. On one memorable occasion I even got seasick while I was snorkeling. As any seasickness-sufferer can testify, we will go to great lengths to avoid bobbing about on any liquid surface. I don't know whether it's karma or just irony that I would end up as part owner of a boat. In any case, I was happy to help Amanda buy it, but I plan to keep appreciating it from afar.

I've always admired Amanda's artistic focus. To be passionate about any pursuit is a gift. As a Yiddish saying goes, "If you have work you love, ask for no other blessing." The child who loved to arrange bits of colored paper became the young woman who won the top award from her college, San Francisco Art Institute. I was in the audience when she won the award and got to feel the fatherly pride of seeing Amanda succeed with her art. My pride was amplified when I learned that the award came with a $2500 cash prize!

When I asked Amanda what she intended to with her new-found wealth, she replied true to form: "Mostly art materials."

I'm the first to admit that I don't understand or even like a lot of the kind of art Amanda does. I love Rembrandt, van Gogh, and a host of other painters. I love Henry Moore, Calder, Louise Nevelson, Brancusi, and many other sculptors. Although Amanda is both a painter and a sculptor, most of her art is conceptual. For example, one of Amanda's pieces that made the newspapers was a clothesline between two San Francisco buildings. She sewed giant-size blue jeans and underwear and hung them across the line high in the sky between two skyscrapers. Even after repeated interviews with the artist herself, I remain largely clueless about the deeper meaning.

However, as Amanda is quick to remind me, "Art doesn't have to mean anything. It just is."

CHAPTER FOURTEEN

CELEBRATING MY BIG BROTHER, MIKE HENDRICKS

Growing up, I was incredibly blessed to have a great older brother, Mike. He was just turning eight when I was born. My mother and he had just weathered the terrible loss of my father, who died while my mother was pregnant with me. Even given that, a picture of him holding me as a baby shows his face lit up with joy.

Most of the memories I have of Mike come from when I was between five and nine years old. After that, he was off in college, and I seldom got to spend time with him. As I reflect on those early years, a steady flow of memories come forth.

Unlike me, Mike has a spectacular ability to build and repair things. I'm hopeless around tools; Mike is a wizard with them. As a kid he built model airplanes and in his teens was always under the hood of some old car he was turning into a hot rod. As a grown-up, he's built three different airplanes by hand and flown them all over the country. A few years ago, when he was almost 80, he bought an ancient Piper Cub, took it apart piece by piece and rebuilt it to like-new specifications.

I remember Mike being patient with me through many failures on my part. One time he built me a model airplane, which I promptly crashed the first time I tried to fly it. Another time he built me a bike with a car steering wheel instead of handlebars, which I also crashed the first time I tried to ride it. He took me on hunting trips with him and let me blast away at squirrels and doves, fortunately with no harm to the creatures. I don't remember ever hitting anything. Once, though, we found a six-foot rattlesnake in our backyard and teamed up to dispatch it with a garden hoe and a machete.

As Mom would always say, Mike and I are "definitely not two peas in a pod." Indeed, we're about as different as two people can be. He was skinny—I was fat. He could fix anything—I break things practically by looking at them. He loves Scotch whiskey and has made many pilgrimages to the Highlands to visit his favorite distilleries. By contrast, I find even the smell of whiskey revolting. As grown-ups, we haven't had the opportunity to spend much time together. We like each other and talk on the phone every month or so, but the fact that we've lived most of our lives on opposite sides of the country has kept us from seeing each other much.

When he graduated with his engineering degree, Mike went to work for NASA. We'd get postcards from the outback of faraway countries where he was engaged in various rocket-related activities. After a few years, he grew tired of the travel and took a job as a trouble-shooting IBM engineer near Washington. He and his wife, Jeanne, built their dream house and settled in with their kids. After a while, he bought a truck and started his own heating and air conditioning repair business, Environmental Systems. When he retired and turned it over to his son, Michael, there were thirty-five of his trucks buzzing around Maryland.

One memory I'll always treasure, even though it came with some pain, was the time we were playing baseball in the sandlot across from our house. I was playing shortstop when the batter hit a sharp grounder in my direction. As I was going for the ball, it struck a rock and flew up to hit me squarely in the forehead. I dropped to all fours, crying in pain, but almost as soon as I hit the ground Mike was right there to help me. He escorted me off the field and took me over to the house to cool off. I remember him showing me my forehead in a mirror, where the stitches of the ball were still imprinted on my skin.

What I remember most, though, was his arm around me as he helped me off the field. It felt so good to have someone to lean on, somebody I could count on always to be by my side, on my side. That was my big brother, Mike Hendricks.

CHAPTER FIFTEEN

THE TWO MOMENTS OF ILLUMINATION THAT CREATED MY CAREER

I saw my first counseling client in 1969, and my latest one yesterday, so at this writing I've been working with people more than 50 years. To date, Katie and I have worked with about 25,000 individuals and couples in our office and seminars, along with 1200 or so C-suite business executives in on-site or office consultations.

Looking back over the whole development of our approach, it divides into three main phases. Phase One goes from 1969 until I met Katie in 1980. In that initial phase, I was focused on finding out how human beings could feel good inside ourselves.

Later, in Phase Two, I expanded into the area of relationships. My questions then centered around how human beings could feel a flow of harmony, love, and creativity in our relations with each other. With Katie as partner, we created the body of relationship work described in *Conscious Loving*, *The Conscious Heart* and several other books.

In Phase Three, I became fascinated by what I call the Genius Zone. I discovered, first in my own life, that human beings are in the Genius Zone when we're doing what we most love to do and what makes our finest contribution to the world around us.

Three book titles express the essence of each phase. The emblematic Phase One book: *Learning to Love Yourself*. In Phase Two: *Conscious Loving*. In Phase Three, *The Big Leap*.

Phase One: Learning to Love Myself

My work in the pre-Katie phase grows out of two life-changing experiences, one in 1969 and the other in 1974. In each of those moments, I learned things experientially that I had never gotten from books, classes, or any traditional learning paradigms. Those two experiences gave me the essential understanding about how human beings can change our lives.

In 1969 I was 24 years old and already making a royal mess of my life. For one thing, I was more than a hundred pounds overweight, a problem I'd carried my whole life. When I was born, my mother was in the midst of the tragedy that would ultimately define her life. My father died suddenly at age 32, within weeks of conceiving me. Due to the stress and turmoil of being suddenly widowed with my seven-year-old brother to take care of, it was several months before my mother realized she was pregnant. The stress of these events threw her into a downward spiral in which she starved herself during the pregnancy from her normal weight of 120 pounds to 89 pounds when I was born. Apparently, her starving threw my hormonal structure off and caused me to gain weight rapidly after my birth, such that by the end of my first year I was in the top 2% of baby weights. By age two, I was visibly fat and for the rest of my childhood was always the "fat kid."

Everybody else in my family was skinny, so I was taken around to many medical specialists to find out what was wrong. I was put on many diets and all sorts of shots and medications were tried out on me, including one memorable year I spent jacked up on amphetamine diet pills. I was in the 9th grade at the time; fueled by the speed, I became a straight-A student, only sinking back to my usual B's and C's when they pulled the plug on the drug.

At age 24, on the day of the experience that would change my life, I not only was carrying more than 100 extra pounds, but I was also in a toxic relationship that was coming apart by the day and working as a teacher and dormitory residential counselor (translation: wrangler) at the school for delinquents I described earlier in the book.

On the fateful day, I stormed out of the apartment to take a walk to clear my head after an argument. I was bundled up against the January cold as I strode along a country road near the school. It had snowed the night before, and I stepped on a patch of ice that was hidden beneath the snow. My feet shot out from under me and I went down with a massive "whump." The back of my head hit the hard road and I actually "saw stars," which up until that moment I thought was a comic-book invention. Fortunately, I didn't hit my head hard enough to knock myself unconscious; in fact, it seemed to have the opposite effect. It knocked me out of my usual perception of myself, and for a couple of minutes I went into a super-conscious state. In that state I learned things about myself that changed the course of my life and took a hundred pounds of extra fat off me. It also gave me an understanding of what causes human unhappiness and a set of change-tools that I would use later with thousands of clients.

In that super-conscious two minutes, I saw dimensions of myself I hadn't been aware of. I could feel how my hundred pounds of extra fat was wrapped around chronically tight muscles, and those tight muscles were clenched around long-buried emotions. The emotions I could suddenly feel in my body were anger, sadness, fear, and shame. I realized I'd been conning myself my whole life by focusing on my fatness: if I worried about being fat all the time, I didn't have to deal with the maelstrom of emotion that was going on underneath the fat. Suddenly, though, in the new state of clarity I could feel anger I'd never been aware of before—anger about not knowing my father, anger at being stuck in a fat body, anger at the overall powerlessness I felt in my life. Deeper in me, I could feel a pool of grief and sadness. I realized I'd been carrying around grief about my father that I'd never acknowledged. I saw how my mother had never recovered from his death, either; she'd turned to a two-pack-a day smoking addiction to cope with her grief, and now the smoking was taking its inevitable toll on her health. I could also still feel the grief from my grandmother's death several years earlier. In that moment on the cold road, I realized I, like Mom, was coping with grief by filling my chest with two packs of distraction every day.

Farther down in my body, beneath the anger clenched in my shoulders and the sadness around my heart, I felt a layer of fear I had never acknowledged. The muscles around my belly felt like a steel belt. There was another sensation in my middle, a speedy swirl of butterflies accompanied by an edge-of-nausea feeling. It was fear, and I realized I'd felt that way as long as I could remember. I kept the feeling at bay by stuffing myself with food to drown out the fear.

Even deeper than the fear was shame, which felt like it spread everywhere in me. Until that moment I don't think I'd ever realized how much shame I carried inside. Lying on the road in that super-conscious state, I saw that the shame in my body was there even before I was born. I didn't understand this perception until years later, when my brother and I were cleaning out my mother's house after her passing. We found an envelope stuck behind a picture in an old frame. It contained an impassioned letter from Mom's church group to her. The note, written in the spidery handwriting of one of the members, begged her to return to the group, not to hide in her house ashamed of her pregnancy. It went on to plead with her that it wasn't her fault life was treating her so cruelly. Please, the letter said, let us support you. My brother and I cried as we read it; we knew she'd never gone back for that support.

I stood with that letter in my hand, almost in a daze, as I realized I'd been pickled in shame from my first origins. It was a low-level hot irritation, like thousands of ants crawling around under my skin. It came with a sense that I'd done something wrong I could never atone for.

As I felt my way down through the layers of unexplored emotion, I made a discovery that would change my life profoundly and give me a foundation for my work. Beneath and beyond all my emotions, I could feel a spacious, oceanic sensation of pure consciousness. It was a shimmering sensation of space and light that was simultaneously at the center of everything and also in the background of everything. In that moment I saw that emotions come and go, but pure consciousness doesn't. It's always there, always on. Pure consciousness is not programmed; it is there before the layers of our history get put on top of it. Since it was deeper than my history, it was the perfect place from which to change my life.

The awareness changed my view of myself and other human beings. I realized that we all get lost in the twisted maze of our minds and the unexplored territory of our emotions, so that we don't get to feel the great reward of the timeless open space that's our true center.

How I got to the state of pure consciousness was also illuminating—by being willing to feel all the anger, sadness, fear, and shame that had previously obscured it. I'd found pure consciousness by going in, down and through, not by going up into my mind or outside myself. I also realized that it was universal, in the sense that everybody had it. It was a natural gift, not something we had to earn or learn.

As I lay there, luxuriating in the space and ease of pure consciousness, I also began to feel my ordinary consciousness coming back. I could feel the gnawing feeling of craving a cigarette, the cold road against my back, and a bunch of dull aches around my body. The sweet sensation of pure conscious-ness was fading from my awareness, but before I lost contact with it, I made a commitment that turned out to affect every moment of my life and work that followed. The commitment: I promise to do everything I can to feel pure consciousness all the time, no matter what I'm doing. That was my promise, to myself and to the universe itself.

I clambered to my feet and set forth for home. Everything was exactly the same, but everything had changed.

The universe must have been listening because it served up the perfect next step for me. On the Sunday following my experience on the ice, I got a call from a friend, Neil Marinello, who asked me if I wanted to go to a talk by his favorite profes-sor when he was a Harvard student. Neil said the professor had recently been to India and had an enlightenment experi-ence that Neil wanted to hear about. He picked me up and we went to Webster Lake, about thirty miles away, where we entered the gates of a beautiful lakeside estate.

The professor, whom Neil had known as Dick Alpert, had changed his name to Ram Dass. I'd heard of him in his old incarnation as Richard Alpert when he made headlines as one of Timothy Leary's LSD adventurers, but I had no idea what to expect. He turned out to be a tall, gangly man dressed in a flowing white robe and surrounded by a coterie of young disciples, all in flowing saris and yoga clothing. I knew nothing about Indian religious traditions or spiritual paths in general, so I didn't have any context for what was going on.

The main event of the afternoon was a talk by Ram Dass, and what a talk it was! Ram Dass sat in a circle of about twenty of us and spoke for three straight hours. What he said was amazing—profound, insightful, often wildly funny—but what really impressed me was that he did it all without any notes. I taught kids from the inner cities of Boston and elsewhere, not always the most eager learners, but even so, I never went into a class without a lesson plan, an outline, and copious notes. Where was he getting all this stuff?

Occasionally, Ram Dass would pause and close his eyes for a while before beginning to speak again. Other times he would pause and look at an 8x10 glossy photo of his guru, a grizzled elder named Neem Karoli Baba.

After the talk, I went over to Ram Dass and asked him two questions. The first one was "Where are you getting this stuff from?" His answer turned my intellectual mind upside down. He said that being around his guru tapped him into a stream of wisdom that had been flowing for thousands of years. All he did was to relax into the stream and open his mouth. The rest took care of itself. That sounded mystifying to me—I was a long way from relaxing into a stream of wisdom and opening my mouth—but the next thing he said radically altered my lifepath and sent me off on a journey I'm still on.

I told Ram Dass about my experience on the ice and asked him point-blank: "What would you recommend I do if I wanted to feel that pure consciousness all the time?" He scanned me up and down, all 300 pounds of me, and said, "In America you might go to therapy, but in India you might meditate, do breathing practices, or physical yoga."

"Where would I learn about that sort of thing?"

"Don't worry," he said, with a dismissive little flap of his hand, "Something will come to you."

A clutch of people were waiting to talk to him, so I thought that perhaps he was just trying to get rid of me. Actually, though, something really did come to me.

The next day, I was in line to check out at a grocery store and looked to my left at a rack of paperback books. One of them almost jumped out at me. It was called *Yoga, Youth and Reincarnation* by Jess Stearn. I snatched the book off the rack and looked at the table of contents. There it was, laid out in one chapter after another: breathing, meditation, yoga postures, chanting, and past lives. It was everything Ram Dass had talked about, except for reincarnation. I don't know what Ram Dass thought about reincarnation, but to me it had always seemed like one of those adult fairy tales, like heaven and hell, that our long-ago ancestors dreamed up to avoid the fear of dying.

I took the book home and worked my way through every exercise in the book, starting in mid-afternoon and ending well after midnight. Somewhere in the wee hours I did the first exercise in the meditation chapter and within a couple of minutes felt the immense space of pure consciousness open up inside me. This time, though, I got to that space sitting on a chair in my living room, not by falling down on an icy road. I was hooked.

In addition to opening a world of new feeling inside me, my new state of consciousness turned out to have a clear practical value. Right away, I started using it to figure out what to eat. Before I ate something, I asked myself, "Will this feed my new body or my old fat body?" I avoided eating anything I'd eaten before my experience on the ice, the steady diet of hamburgers, hot dogs, and ice cream that led to my size 48 trousers (instead of the size 34 I wear now, fifty years later). One of my biggest discoveries in my new way of eating were those amazing things called fruits and vegetables, things I almost never ate in my former life. It wasn't long before a bowl of blueberries turned me on as much or more than a bowl of ice cream had in my old life.

Over the next year, I lost on the average a couple of pounds a week. During that first year of radical change, I encountered a phenomenon I began to call the Upper Limit Problem. An Upper Limit Problem (or, as our students call it, an ULP) is when you sabotage yourself when things are going well. An ULP is like an allergic response to success, based on old limiting beliefs about yourself such as "I don't deserve to be successful."

I noticed my first ULP a month or so after I started eating the new way. Switching from a burger and ice cream diet to one based on fruits and vegetables caused weight to fall off me rapidly, more than a pound a day. I'd dropped almost forty pounds when one day I found myself gazing lustfully through the window of Brigham's Ice Cream shop in Cambridge, Mass. Inside, a family of four was devouring a huge banana split. It looked so good that, as my grandmother used to say, I "lost my religion." It was like I went into a trance and got magnetically pulled into the store, where I pointed to the giant banana split and said, "Give me one of those, please." I remember the clerk looking over my shoulder to see where the rest of my party was. I was the sole party, though, and for the next half hour I spooned, gorged, and slurped my way through the whole works, complete with three scoops of ice cream and a banana, all doused in chocolate, butterscotch, and caramel sauce and topped, of course, with generous dollops of whipped cream.

I staggered out of the place sugar-drunk and bloated. For twenty minutes or so, while the massive sugar rush led cheers in my bloodstream, all was just fine in the world. Then, ten blocks down the street, I got hit by a stomach ache so bad that I doubled over in pain right there on the street. (This happened only twice in my life and both of them were memorable and turned out to be important wake-up calls.) A few compassionate passersby said, "Are you okay?"

I said I was, but I definitely wasn't. I was in the grip of the Upper Limit Problem. I had apparently arrived at the limit of my tolerance for feeling good and had committed sabotage-by-sundae.

There is nothing better than a gut-punch belly ache and feeling miserable for three days to make a vivid impression on even the most awareness-resistant person. That's what it took to bring my self-sabotage script to light. I got the message, though, and went back to my new way of eating.

A year and a lot of broccoli later, I was down to about 200 pounds, with more coming off over the next few years. (Over the past ten years I've been around 180 pounds, which on my six-foot frame feels like a good weight.)

I also kicked two other major addictions, a two-pack-a-day Marlboro habit and a tendency to get involved in unfulfilling relationships. My particular specialty in the area of relationships was to get involved with women who were struggling with addictions.

Hmm. where would I have gotten that idea? Any Psych 101 student could have probably told me it had something to do with my early experiences with my mother, but that insight had not penetrated my awareness yet.

At the time of my slip on the ice, I was in a relationship with a woman who would later get sober through Alcoholics

Anonymous. At the time I knew her, though, most of her drinking was done in secret. I was so oblivious and caught up in my own dramas that I didn't notice the extent to which alcohol was affecting our lives. In another relationship, I fell for a woman who was relaxed and fun to be around most of the time but would suddenly go into dark moods for days at a time. Then she'd brighten up again and things would go well for a while. After a few months of trying to deal with the fluctuations, I discovered that she had a secret source for the wildly popular new "miracle drug," Valium. Sometimes the source would dry up and dark moods would ensue.

Fortunately, I woke up from that particular trance and ended up marrying the woman of my dreams. That would come later, though, and I don't want to minimize the pain involved in extracting myself from the entanglement of toxic relationships. I kicked cigarettes by grinding my way through three days of miserable body sensations but getting out of my old relationship patterns—particularly the one about saving addicts from themselves—was a process that took years.

The effect of this experience on my work was profound. It gave me a new model of human beings that turned out to have enormous therapeutic power. I saw how we are arranged in layers of inner experience, just as we are arranged in physical layers of skin, fat, organs, and blood. Proceeding down the body from the top, we have a layer of mind, the repository of thoughts, beliefs, memories, and language. Below our minds, we all have several layers of emotion and sensation, including the anger that fires up muscles in our back, neck and jaws, the sadness that constricts our chest and puts a lump in our throat, the fear that stops our digestion and causes "butterflies" in the stomach. There are hunger sensations in our bellies and further down in the pelvis the compelling currents of our sexuality.

At the center of everything, as I discovered on the icy road, is the natural gift of our pure consciousness. We get to this exalted space by allowing ourselves to experience and accept all the other phenomena inside us, such as our feelings. Peace of mind was really peace of body, and the only way to feel it came through directing our awareness inward, rather than outward. This idea was the therapeutic game-changer for me. From then on, whenever I worked with people, I always knew that their ultimate freedom came from being aware of the layers of experience within themselves, especially the spacious openness of pure consciousness.

The F-A-C-T Algorithm: A Powerful Transformational Tool

The experience that began on my back on an icy country road led me to develop an algorithm that sped up and deepened the transformational process. An algorithm is a formula that makes a complex task simple, repeatable, and fast. For example, my most successful investment during the dot.com era of the 90s was a Santa Barbara start-up, Software.com, built around a tiny algorithm, a formula that made it possible to send bigger and faster emails. Older readers may remember a time when email was clunky and often crashed if you sent big attachments. Software.com solved that problem, and after it went public it ended up with a market cap of several billion dollars. I found it astonishing that a strip of computer code could be worth as much as a company that made something "real" like shoes or cars.

I have found the F-A-C-T Algorithm to be that kind of useful. Here's how it works:

F stands for Facing.
A stands for Accepting and Loving.
C stands for Choosing.
T stands for Taking Action.

The first step in resolving any issue is to face it squarely as it is. A good friend of mine told me that one moment of facing something squarely changed his life: "My name is John and I'm an alcoholic." Until that day, if anybody suggested he had a drinking problem, as a succession of friends, wives, and former bosses had done, he replied with a defensive "I can handle it."

Once you've faced something, the next crucial step is to accept and love it as it is. That step can take ten seconds or ten years, because it all depends on your willingness. I've seen people shed a lifetime of pain in a brief moment of loving acceptance. I've also seen people dig in and refuse to accept something about themselves, so that they delay their growth for years.

Choosing and taking effective action can only come from facing and accepting something unconditionally in yourself. Choosing what you want and what action you want to take to get it becomes much easier when you're coming from a state of inner harmony.

Although each of the four steps are important, all of them depend on the first step of Facing. For example, once a client has described a problem to me, one of the first questions I ask is, "What about all of this is hardest to face?" Often, the thing that must be faced is in the world of emotion. Fundamental feelings such as anger, fear and sadness are hard to face for many people because of their early programming. In some families, anger is the taboo emotion that must not be expressed. In other families the prohibition is against the expression of sadness ("Big boys don't cry") or fear ("There's nothing to be scared about.") By the time we get to adulthood most of us have developed walls between us and certain emotions. Facing them becomes an important part of our lifework.

Facing feelings means feeling them. Since the sensations of each emotion are in the body, here we run up against another wall of prohibition: difficulty in being aware of key body-sensations. For example, a client is talking about anxiety. When I as a body-oriented question such as "Where do you feel anger in your body?", the person is often unable to answer the question. How could that be? Imagine if I asked the same person, "How does your body lets you know you need to go to the bathroom?" Most people would be able to describe the sensations readily. Why would anger, fear and sadness be harder to describe than the urge to visit the bathroom?

I think the answer is simple. We get a tremendous amount of practice at an early age in recognizing the need to go to the bathroom. The essential skills are explained over and over to us, and we get massive encouragement as we learn. Contrast that with how little careful training we get on how to recognize the sensations of anger, fear or sadness. Most of us have mastered toilet training by the time we're in pre-school. I know for a fact, though, that people can get all the way through college without knowing how to recognize core emotions such as anger and fear. I was one of those people.

It may be different now, but I didn't get any training in emotional literacy until I was in graduate school. Given how much of life depends on the ability to handle emotional situations, failure to teach people how to deal with them constitutes, in my view, educational malpractice. I remember spending time in elementary school memorizing the capitals of South

American countries, a body of knowledge I have yet to draw on. Imagine if the equivalent amount of time had been spent showing us how to navigate the world of our emotions.

Once you have faced something, the next move is to accept it. Accepting takes you deeper inward than facing. Using the example of fear, the goal is to face and accept the fear so deeply that you feel the open space of pure consciousness that lies beneath and beyond all our emotions. The ultimate form of accepting is to love something as it is, to let go and let it be. Then, from that space, which is uncluttered by your past programming, you can make a choice and act on it.

Pause for a moment to experience what acceptances actually feels like. Think of what day it is where you are at the moment. It happens to be Wednesday where I am right now, so let's use that day as an example. Feel how easy it is to accept whatever day it is where you are. Notice how little resistance or argument you have about what day of the week it is. Even if you don't like some of the things you might be doing on that particular day, notice that you don't usually think, "Damn that Wednesday—why does it even exist? I'm not going to accept Wednesdays from now on!"

For example, facing that you're scared about something is an important step, but accepting your fear takes you into deeper territory. When you accept something, you welcome it into the wholeness of yourself. It's no longer something "out there." You've brought it inside. That's a good thing, because once you've welcomed it into your field of awareness, you can use the energy of it to fuel your journey to your chosen goals.

Once you have faced and deeply accepted the reality of something, you are poised to take the last two steps of the FACT algorithm, Choosing and Taking Action. Knowing this algorithm is useful for healers of any kind, because it gives you a framework for transformation. Most people who come to us for help are having a problem with these two latter steps, Choosing and Taking Action. Working backward from there, problems with Choosing and Taking Action are occurring because something hasn't been Faced and Accepted. Choosing and Taking Action become easy and natural once one has Faced and Accepted the block that's been prevent choice and action.

One of the most surprising lessons of my early years was that emotions are simply energy in motion. Like many people, I had grown up with a lot of programmed resistance to my feelings. "Boys don't cry" was the dominant level of emotional intelligence in the John Wayne era I grew up in. The way to be a man was to pretend you didn't have any emotions but anger. It was okay to express anger; on the average there was at least one fistfight every week among my boyhood cronies. By contrast, I can only remember one incident when any of us cried or showed any emotion but anger. I got hit in the forehead by a baseball and was escorted off the field in tears by my older brother, with him hissing in my ear to stop crying.

The discovery that feelings are "energy in motion" turned out to be genuinely useful; it allowed me to get underneath all the things I'd been taught to think about my feelings. For example, once I opened my awareness to directly feel the shimmering, dancing energy that made up fear in my belly, it wasn't scary anymore. It was simply energy moving from place to place to send me a message. In the case of fear, the message is that, for some reason, my body is experiencing a threat of some kind. I say "for some reason" because the threat may be an external one, such as a surprise sight of a bear on your back porch (which actually happens fairly often in our small town.) More often, though, the threats come from inside us, in the form of thoughts we manufacture to our own design.

For example, I had a boss once I didn't get along with. I made him out to be rigid and authoritarian, which many of my co-workers also found him to be. However, I seemed to bring out the worst of him, leading to repeated conflicts between us. One magic day, though, everything changed. What brought about the change was a therapy-assisted insight that ended the conflict.

The therapist pointed out that I had grown up without a father and had a chip on my shoulder about it. She also showed me that there was a layer of fear underneath my anger, the fear of not knowing how to connect with men and get my needs met. She suggested that I let myself feel my anger, fear, and grief about not ever knowing my father, as an alternative to aiming my hostility at the father figure of my boss.

As you probably already guessed, my boss changed overnight! Once I got my mis-aimed anger out of the way, I got along with him much better. He and I didn't become friends, but at least we got so we could carry out a disagreement without yelling at each other. Absence of yelling isn't the only metric by which to grade the merits of a conversation, but it's a pretty good start.

Phase Two: Into the World of Relationships

By the late '70s I had developed a reliable toolkit for relieving emotional pain and creating good feelings on the inside. As I enjoyed more of a flow of good feeling inside myself, I became more acutely aware that one major area of my life caused most of the pain: my relationships. I made a vow to learn as much as I could about relationships, so I could create a lasting, loving one for myself. As I got my attention fully on the subject, I quickly found that learning about relationships is learning about projection.

Discovering the Power of Projection

Projection is when you see a negative quality or feeling in someone else that's actually in *you*. Have you ever accused someone of lying to you, only to realize you'd been lying to them about something? I've done that one. Have you ever thought another person didn't like you, only to realize that deep down inside you didn't really like them? I've done that one, too. A classic moment of breaking through my projections changed the whole direction of my relationship life. Go back through time with me to a crisp autumn day in 1973.

I'm walking down a street in San Francisco, with my then-girlfriend, Jen. I'm 28 years old, and she's my third girlfriend since I arrived in California in 1971. Although we haven't come right out and said it, we're wondering if we should call it quits. We've been seeing each other for six months or so, and after the initial rush of sexual attraction subsided, we've been in a holding pattern.

We're not getting any closer, but we haven't split up and moved on. I've had pretty much the same complaints about her all along, and she's had hers about me.

My big complaint is that she's too critical—of herself and me and everything else in the world. Hers is that I'm emotionally distant and never talk about anything important, such as my feelings.

As we walk along, making small talk—carefully avoiding talking about what we really ought to be talking about—I'm carrying on a silent conversation in my head about why I always seem to get stuck with critical women who don't really seem to care about me. I'm mentally muttering something like, *Of all the three billion women in the world, why do I always seem to get stuck with the critical ones? Why do they always seem to seek me out?* As if by magic, Jen starts talking about what she doesn't like about her job. It's the same things she always doesn't like about her job.

I mention that she's complained about all this before. Then she starts telling me all the things that are wrong with me, including one of the big things, which is that I'm always complaining about her complaining. I've heard them all before, but she seems just as excited to tell me all the things that are wrong with me as the first few dozen times she told me. I tune her out and begin wondering about how I managed to create this kind of situation in my life.

A Glimmer of Awareness: The Rule of Three

As Jen and I walk along, lost in our own worlds, a glimmer of something new flickers in the edge of my awareness. Jen is my third girlfriend in a row who has the characteristic of being hyper-critical. I'm a Ph.D. student in the Stanford counseling psychology program; the program is heavily research-oriented, and as such, I'm immersed in statistics day and night. My statistics brain fires up with a basic statistics rule: it only takes three data points to predict a trend. As I think about it, I realize that if I go back to my teenage years, I've had far more than three critical girlfriends. Like an AA member standing up in front of the room for the first time, I humbly realize that I've got a critical girlfriend trend going. The numbers tell me something I can't believe I hadn't seen before: I pick women who criticize me a lot.

Up until this moment I'd always assumed it was the woman's problem, that I was just an innocent bystander in a world of critical women. In other words, I'd always perceived myself as the victim of their critical natures. Now, this tiny flicker of awareness opens up a new doorway of possibility. Maybe the pattern has something to do with me!

The Benign Jolt, The Blissful Aftermath

Suddenly I'm gifted with a rapid-fire series of insights. Where they come from, I'll never know. It's like a bolt of enlightenment giving me a benign but unforgettable jolt. I feel immense peace, clarity, and zest stream into my body and mind as the realization settles into me.

Here's the insight that brought me (and still brings me) that remarkable feeling of serenity and aliveness:

1. The results I create tell me what my true intentions are. My results tell me that I've had a series of relationships with women I complain are critical.

2. I have critical women in my life because I have an intention to have a critical woman in my life. That intention is obviously stronger than any intention I have to be in relationship with a loving, supportive woman.

3. The intention has been entirely unconscious. It's been so hidden from me that if someone an hour before had asked, "Do you intend to have a critical woman in your life?" I would have proclaimed self-righteously, "That's utterly ridiculous. My intention is to have a loving, supportive woman in my life. I just keep getting stuck with women who are critical."

4. I face the sober truth: I'm getting exactly what I intend to get, and just because the intention is unconscious doesn't mean it's not my intention. I quickly extend this profoundly unsettling insight to two other things I complain about all the time: my weight and my money supply.

5. I'm overweight. That's the result I'm producing. Therefore, I obviously have an unconscious intention to be fat. My intention to be fat is more powerful than my intention to be healthy.

6. I'm chronically short of money. That's the result I'm creating. Therefore, I obviously have an unconscious intention to be poor.

As these insights illuminate my mind, I can hear a little voice in my mind shrieking, "No, no, please don't let that be true!" It's so much easier to blame society for my poverty. It's so much easier to portray myself as the victim of the fat-genes I inherited. If I went to a meeting of fat people, I'd have a crowd around me if I started a conversation about inheriting fat-genes from my ancestors. If I went to a meeting of poor people, I'd get an enthusiastic response if I talked about how society and "the system" make us poor.

I wonder, though, what kind of reception I would get if I said, "Hey, everybody, gather around! Let's talk about how we all have unconscious intentions to be fat!"

What would happen if I made the same announcement to my impoverished friends? "Hey, let's stop complaining about being poor and blaming it on anything. Let's figure out why we have unconscious intentions to stay poor!" Would I get out of the room alive?

I quickly realized, though, that it didn't matter what anybody else thought. The moment I quit blaming my genes and started claiming my own unconscious intention to be fat, I felt a new and unusual sense of aliveness in my body. It felt like I was waking up from a long and painful trance, coming out of a stuffy room to breathe fresh air. There was no arguing with the zest I could feel when I took responsibility instead of blaming anyone or anything. There was no arguing with the delicious feeling of serenity that was settling into my mind and body.

The new awareness eliminated the need for any kind of complicated therapy process. Whenever any problem arose, all I had to do was claim the unconscious intention for that problem. All I had to do was find out where this old intention was rooted and replace it with a new conscious intention.

The results you create tell you what your true intentions are! That insight made everything utterly simple. For example, if I say my intention is to be sober but I just got a DUI, my true intention is to drink. If you say your intention is to love and honor your mate but three of your last mates say they left you because you abused them, your true intention is not to honor and love them.

A Second Flash of Illumination

Another lightning-bolt of insight lit up my mind. It answered a key question: How can I tell when an unconscious intention is running me?

I realized that the quick way to find my unconscious intentions was to notice what I complain about repetitively. For example, I complained to many girlfriends about their criticism. I thought their criticalness was the problem. Only later did I discover that I had an unconscious intention to hook up with critical women.

The same insight applied to my weight. I had complained about my weight—and my powerlessness to do anything about it—since I was a kid, only to discover that I had an unconscious intention to be fat.

I eventually developed another algorithm that I call the "Rule of Three": Anything about myself that I complain about three or more times is actually driven by an unconscious intention.

The Rule of Three brought me many moments of lifechanging awareness. Sometimes they were downright weird, but they were always useful. For example, I complained more than three times (probably more like 300 times!) about people lighting up cigarettes near me. One incident stands out in my memory, from the days before smoking was banned in airports.

I was waiting for a plane in the Colorado Springs airport, and as was my custom, I had placed myself in the Non-Smoking area. In fact, I was standing right under the sign that said Non-Smoking Area. A thin, nervous-looking woman, perhaps 65 years of age, walked up, stood right beside me, and started rummaging through her purse. She pulled out a pack of cigarettes, shook one out, and lit it up. Thinking perhaps she hadn't seen the sign, I said politely, "Excuse me, you can't smoke here." I pointed to the sign above our heads. She glared furiously at me and said, "I'll smoke anywhere I g****m please."

Her flash of rage startled me, but when I recovered, I got angry and lost any urge to be polite. "No, you can't," I said, "This is the non-smoking area, and if you don't put it out, I'll go get a cop to explain it to you."

Here's where it took a turn toward the bizarre. "You idiot," she hissed, pronouncing it "idjit." She said, "My husband just died. Nobody's going to tell me I can't smoke." This response was so strange and unexpected that all I could do was stand there, slack-jawed, in a trance. I slunk away and stood somewhere else.

Later I told this story to Katie, who pointed out something that changed my life.

She said, "That's amazing, honey, but that's your karma, isn't it?"

I told her I didn't understand what she meant.

She said, "Well, given your past, think about why you might attract a situation like that."

I still didn't get it, so she continued, "Didn't you spend your entire early existence with a woman who smoked incessantly because she was angry that her husband had just died?"

That observation rocked my world. Could the power of unconscious intention be that strong? As I explained earlier in the book, my father died a few weeks after conceiving me. My mother was naturally devastated by his death, and she also did not know yet that she was pregnant with me. According to the family stories, she lived mostly on coffee and cigarettes for several months after my father's death, dropping from her normal weight of 120 pounds to under 90 pounds. Then, she finally realized she was pregnant and went into a deep depression.

In other words, I spent my first months of existence inside a heavy smoker who was starving herself to death out of grief and anger about her husband's death. She had no job, my older brother to take care of, and $300 to her name.

Could this set of early experiences have set in motion a powerful unconscious intention to attract critical female smokers into my life? Could a childhood imprint be so powerful that it would cause me to draw a grief-stricken, angry smoker up next to me in a non-smoking area? At first it seemed preposterous to my scientific mind, but then I recalled another incident that eerily followed the same pattern.

I participated in a seminar some years ago, one of many I did in the 70s and 80s. During one process, we were asked to sit across from a partner for a communication exercise. We were each given sixty seconds to tell our partner about a painful breakdown of communication during our early lives. The instructor told us to sit in silence, just making eye contact with each other, for a few moments before we began. My partner seemed incredibly nervous. Her eyes were darting around so much I could never make eye contact with her. I also noticed she was fiddling with something down in her lap. When the instructor told us to start our sixty seconds of communication, she said "You go first."

Now for the weird part. The incident I dredged up to tell her about had to do with trying to communicate with my mother while she was smoking or craving a cigarette. Mom was a newspaper columnist who did a lot of her writing in the early morning hours. Every day I woke to a houseful of cigarette smoke, the staccato clack of Mom's old Underwood typewriter and the hack of her smoker's cough. Both of us knew the smoking was killing her, which it ultimately did, but she was never able kick the addiction.

As I poured my story out to my twitchy partner, I suddenly caught sight of what she was fiddling with in her hands. It was an unlit cigarette! She was rolling it in her fingers, even caressing it. I was stunned. When my sixty seconds were up and it was my partner's turn, she abruptly jumped to her feet and said "I've got to go." She raced out of the room and, even though it was only halfway through the weekend workshop, she never came back.

What are the odds against telling a story about my childhood difficulties with a tobacco addict to a stranger who was craving a smoke? The only satisfying explanation was to acknowledge the power of unconscious intention based on primal experiences. Now, with half a century of working with people under my belt, I see much more clearly how the phenomenon works.

Early life experiences create templates for how life has to be. For example, Tiger Woods grew up around a father who was chronically unfaithful to his wife. Is it any surprise that Tiger would later blow up his life with infidelity? Similarly, I know a guy who spent his prenatal life nurtured by tobacco-saturated nutrients and later fell in love with a woman who smoked. I happen to know a lot about that guy, because he is me. Not only did I as a twenty-something fall in love with a tobacco addict, I spent a lot of time and energy over the next couple of years trying to get her to quit.

What drives us to create one unsatisfying experience after another that resemble unsatisfying early childhood patterns? I felt incomplete in my early nurturing needs, so it drove me into one relationship after another with a woman who struggled with addiction.

The most important value of claiming an unconscious intention is that you can put a conscious one in its place. I set a new intention: to create a relationship that was completely loving and supportive, free of any pattern of criticism. I added a further commitment never to attract another addict into my life. I'm happy to tell you that both of those commitment produced the best possible results. The proof is my 40+ years of marriage to a loving, supportive womanoo who is blessedly free of addicti.ons. Early in our relationship we made a agreement to eliminate criticism and blame from our marriage. It took us a few years to make good on that commitment, but it was well worth the effort. It's been decades now since either of us has said any kind of critical word to the other.

That's the power of *conscious* intention.

In Practice

Beware of blaming or criticizing yourself for having unconscious intentions. It's not a fault, a flaw, or anything negative. It just is, and the quicker we acknowledge it, the quicker we get our peace of mind and zest for living back.

Instead of blaming yourself, make an innocent self-inquiry by wondering "How did I come to have an intention like that?"

Another way to ask that question is: "Given my background, where might I have picked up an unconscious intention like that?"

I've had thousands of conversations that contain some version of the following interchange.

Client: Are you saying that I may have an unconscious intention to get sick a lot?

Me: Yes. The results always tell you what your true intentions are. You've taken all your sick days for the year and it's only March. Given your background, where might you have picked up an intention to spend so much time feeling ill?

This example is a client who got sick a lot, but it could easily be a number of other symptoms: having frequent accidents, failing repeatedly, being obese, practicing addictions. They are all based on unconscious intentions that must be acknowledged in order to be released.

Eventually, the person makes the connection and sees exactly where the unconscious intention became glued into place. The first step in ungluing it is simply to acknowledge and claim it instead of being defensive about it.

Our lives are shaped by our intentions, but many of those intentions are unconscious and based on old programming. Inevitably, those unconscious intentions produce unsatisfying results. All of us, at all times, and in every way, are getting exactly what we intend to get. There is no better place to study this phenomenon than in close relationships.

Early in our marriage, Katie and I discovered the only quick and foolproof way to find out our true intentions: look at the results we produced. For example, even if we think we're committed to spending more quality time together, a quick look at the results will tell us whether we're genuinely committed to it. If we're not spending more quality time together, we have to admit that we're not actually committed to it. The results tell us our intention is not to spend quality time with each other. Then, the question becomes "Why would we be having that intention right now?" Ask that question with wonder, not blame, and you will be rewarded with rapid, life-changing insights.

Come into a session with us. That way you can see how these principles work in the heat of action. As you watch this drama unfold, you may think that it is moving far more quickly and easily than work with troubled relationships often does. To present a clear example of the principles, we selected a transcript in which the work does indeed proceed relatively smoothly. As any experienced therapist knows, however, there are often bumps along the way.

Our clients, I'll call them Maria and Ed, have made the journey from Chicago to work with us for two days. Their surface complaints with each other may have a familiar ring to them. From Ed's perspective, the problem is very simple: Maria is stingy with sex. Maria hears this with a snort of disgust. From her perspective the problem is emotional distance. Ed rolls his eyes—they've been there before. "When we were first married we made love every day," he says. "Now I'm lucky if it's every other week. That doesn't work for me."

Maria doesn't sympathize at all with Ed's sexual frustration. "I need more connection with you if I'm going to get turned on. You can't go around emotionally detached all day Saturday then suddenly get physical with me at bedtime. When we were first together you seemed interested in me as a person, not just a body."

As therapists, our first task is to find out if they are both committed to solving the problem. Although they've come a long way and paid a considerable fee, we need to hear a clear "yes" before we can get anything meaningful done. People come to couples-counseling for many reasons other than to make breakthrough discoveries about themselves that will open the flow of more love. Some have hidden agendas such as proving that the marriage is really hopeless.

Our way of flushing out those hidden agendas is to ask them blunt questions.

Our first question is designed to help us find out if they are genuinely committed to solving the problem: "Are you willing to do whatever it takes to resolve these issues so you can feel more love flowing between you?"

They stare and blink.

Ed finally breaks the silence: "We're here, aren't we?" he says, a trace of sarcasm in his voice.

"We hear your irritation," we say, "but please note that you didn't say "Yes."

"I don't get it," he says.

Ed's a real estate developer, so we use a real estate metaphor: "If you asked a couple if they wanted to buy a house they liked, what would happen if they said, 'We're here, aren't we?' Would you consider that the same commitment as a "Yes" or a signature?"

He gets the point. Maria's already got the point. Still, she can't resist tossing a barb in Ed's direction.

"That's the Ed I call Mr. Smart-Ass."

Noting the clenching of his jaw, we invite them to take a few deep breaths, then ask them our original question again.

This time they both say "Yes." That's all we need. It doesn't matter if they have a dozen murky agendas—practically everybody does. It doesn't matter if they have a ton of resistance and two tons of transference. All that matters is that they go on record with a clear "Yes." With a clear commitment to do everything possible to solve the problem, everyone has a firm place to stand on.

There's a change in the energy in the room. Although we're talking about heavy issues, the energy is lighter, more charged. Commitment has that effect—it puts a kind of benign electricity in the air.

Next, we ask them to make the briefest possible statement about the problem, and to direct the statement to each other, not to us.

"I'm not getting enough sex," Ed says.

"I'm not getting enough emotional connection with you," Maria says.

"Okay," we say, "Now we're going to use our most powerful technique to help you solve this problem. Still want us to do that?"

They say "Yes."

Then we say, "The best way to find out your real intentions is to observe the results you're producing. Like, if an alcoholic says his intention is to be sober, the best way to find out if that's his true intention is to find out if he's had a drink recently.

"So, Ed," we say, "Look Maria in the eye and say 'My intention is to not get enough sex.'"

His face turns red, and he explodes with a loud "WHAT?"

We explain: "You say you're not getting enough sex, and the results always tell you what your true intentions are. So just tell her, 'Maria, I have an intention to not have enough sex.'"

He whips his head from side to side. "No, no, no—I'm telling you my intention is to have plenty of sex. How could I be committed to not getting enough sex?"

We say, "That's a good question. Let's come back to that. In the meantime, notice that you're avoiding looking Maria in the eye. You're avoiding saying, 'Maria, I'm committed to not having enough sex.'"

"Even if I don't believe it?" he asked.

We nod. "Just say it. Accent the word "not.""

"Maria, I'm committed to not having enough sex."

Although his face still looks puzzled and doubtful, we note that his breathing shifts to become deeper and easier.

Now it's her turn. "Maria, look Ed in the eye and say, 'Ed, I'm committed to not having an emotional connection with you anymore.'"

It's clear that enlightenment has already dawned on Maria. She nods as she says, "Ed, I'm committed to not having an emotional connection with you anymore."

"Why?" he asks plaintively. Suddenly there's a younger tone in his voice, a kind of innocence he's been covering over with hostility.

We say, "Let's wonder about that together. Ed, where would you have gotten the idea that you were supposed to live in a marriage where you didn't make love as often as you wanted? Maria, where would you have gotten the idea that you were supposed to be emotionally distant from your husband?"

Maria has already figured it out; Ed's shaking his head in puzzlement. We give him a prompt. "Does that remind you of any relationships you saw around you growing up? Were there any people you saw frequently who complained about sexual frustration?"

He barks a sharp, bitter laugh. "My parents fought about that constantly. I probably heard my old man bitch about his crappy sex life about five hundred times a year."

Maria chimes in with a similar observation. "My father and my brothers are all so cool and distant. I'm the only person in my family I've ever seen cry. Good providers, but like there's nobody home inside."

"So," we reflect back, "You both learned by osmosis that marriage is supposed to be full of sexual frustration and emotional distance."

"Looks like it, doesn't it," Ed says.

"Want to make a commitment to changing that?" we ask. They say "yes."

The magic begins the moment you spot and acknowledge your unconscious intentions. That very act is the main thing you need to do to change the pattern. For example, let's say you're supposed to give a presentation on Tuesday morning. You wake up at dawn with a sore throat, so you call in to work and cancel the presentation. The magic begins the moment you realize and acknowledge your unconscious intention: "The results tell me that my true intention is to avoid giving the presentation."

The act of acknowledging your unconscious commitments frees up creative energy to wonder, "Hmmm, why might I want to avoid giving the presentation?"

If you ask that question with sincere intent, the reasons often reveal themselves rapidly. There's almost always more than one reason. It's usually a short stack of reasons, such as "I want to avoid it because I don't feel prepared" or "I want to avoid it because I'm afraid of the reaction to some of the stuff in the presentation." Claiming your unconscious intention is one of the ways you make rapid progress in life. Your progress screeches to a halt when you get defensive and argue that your real intention is to give the presentation—it's just bad timing that you got sick that day. The defensive position boils down to "I didn't have anything to do with my sore throat."

I've worked for fifty years now with the art of consciously claiming responsibility for previously unconscious intentions. In our seminars, I've led more than twenty thousand people through the process of reclaiming their power through owning their unconscious intentions. Even though I've seen it many times, it always moves me deeply. Being with people as they step out of the victim position and into the full power of their creative energy is one of life's greatest experiences.

Here's my summary advice on using this principle in your daily life: Keep it simple and you'll move very quickly. Just notice any negative result you're producing and claim the unconscious intention to produce that result.

Keeping it simple resulted in my one and only ten-minute therapy session. A businessman in his thirties came in for his first session. He explained that he had some kind of upper limit on his income. He would get close to breaking $200,000 a year, then would do something to sabotage himself so that he never quite made it. In the latest episode, he'd been up near $200,000 but then suffered a $76,000 loss that knocked him back down to the zone where he usually resided.

I gave him a two-minute explanation of how unconscious intention works and asked him to declare the intention out loud. He didn't hesitate a beat. He said, "My intention is to never make more than $200,000."

"Why do you think you might have an intention like that?"

He shook his head in amazement. "Why didn't I think of this before? It's about my dad. We're in business together, and I know he has never made more than $200,000 a year. If I made more than that, I'd show him up."

"Sounds like you may have cracked the code."

He spread his hands in a gesture of wonder.

"Damn," he said, "That's amazing." He shook his head and again wondered aloud why he hadn't thought of it before.

Then I explained that right after you claim an unconscious intention is the perfect time to put a new conscious one into place—to ask yourself: What would I like instead?

I invited him to set a new intention, by saying the following sentences over a few times:

"It's okay to make more than Dad."

"The more money I make the happier Dad gets."

"I make money to please me and nobody else."

After he finished, he glanced at his watch. "What do we for the rest of the hour?"

"Go take your dad out for coffee and tell him what you just learned."

I never saw him professionally again, but a year or so later I saw him and his wife across the street while walking downtown. He gave me a thumbs-up signal and shouted over to me above the noise, "$237,000!"

I gave him a thumbs-up back and pointed up to the sky, as in "The sky's the limit."

He got it and bobbed his head in agreement.

Colorado Breakthrough

In 1974 I made a breakthrough that brought about a quantum difference in the results I got with my clients. The event is documented in detail in my book, *Learning to Love Yourself*. For our purposes here I'll tell a brief version of the story and focus on the practical application of the lesson I got from the experience.

I had a goal of completing my Ph.D. before I was 30 and then looking for a university job training counselors and therapists. I visualized an academic career at a major university, where I would teach and have freedom to write and conduct research. In 1974 the first half of my dream came true, getting my Ph.D. when I was turning 29, with a year and 16 days to spare!

Later that same year, the second half of my dream manifested when I was offered the position of assistant professor at the University of Colorado. The salary was $13,000, which after three years of living on $300/month graduate student budget felt like a fortune to me. I moved from Palo Alto to Colorado in August of 1974, slated to teach my first graduate school class in September.

There's an old saying about being careful what you wish for … because you just might get it. I experienced the truth of it not long after I arrived in Colorado. I found a beautiful mountain cabin in Green Mountain Falls for what seemed like a ridiculously low rent. (After California, everything in Colorado seemed like a bargain!) I moved in two weeks before school started and spent my days getting to know my surroundings.

The leaves of the aspen trees on the hillsides were turning their bright yellow fall color. I'd never seen aspens before. The locals called them "quaking" aspen because of the way the leaves shimmered in the wind. When the sun shone on the leaves it looked like the foothills were illuminated by flickering yellow lights.

As the day of my first class was fast approaching, I went out for a morning walk, and instead of enjoying the brisk air of a Colorado autumn, I had an anxiety attack. A massive wave of doubt swept over me. One moment I was strolling along in perfect harmony, when suddenly a particular chain of thoughts triggered a gut-gripping panic. The doubtful thoughts culminated in this conclusion:

"I'm about to teach my first graduate class at a major university and I don't know ANYTHING."

The logical part of my mind knew that was ridiculous. I knew everything the books and scientific studies had to say about my subject. I was well-trained in all the major techniques of counseling and psychotherapy. When I said I didn't know "anything," what I meant was I didn't know ONE thing. I wanted to know the one thing we humans do that gets us stuck in cycles of unhappiness, and the one thing we can do to get ourselves free. I had a conviction that there must be one crucial, erroneous move we humans make that takes us into the realm of misery. Likewise, there must be one thing we can do to reclaim the happiness I felt was our birthright.

I didn't know what that one thing was, and I felt the lack intensely.

It was the quest for that one thing that first drove me to start my master's degree at University of New Hampshire and then go on for my doctorate at Stanford. Now I'd gone to the peak of higher education, and I still hadn't found the answer.

You may be thinking, "Well, maybe there isn't a 'one thing.' Get over it." I certainly wouldn't blame you, because I had that thought myself about a dozen times a day.

Looking back on it from the perspective of four decades later, I can see how absurd it was to place that kind of expectation on myself at 29. I'm glad I did, though, because through the vehicle of an anxiety attack, I discovered what I'd been looking for.

Standing under the canopy of trees on that crisp autumn day of 1974, I felt waves of anxiety coursing up from my belly, making me feel slightly nauseous. Suddenly, though, I had a flash of illumination: I had been asking the right question, but I'd been asking it the wrong way! I don't know where that insight came from, but it changed my life and has continued to do so for almost 50 years.

I realized I'd always pursued my quest intellectually, by seeking knowledge outside myself, in the form of books, courses, and degrees. The one thing I'd never done was to take the questions inside:

What did I do to make myself unhappy?

What could I do to get free?

So, right there on the spot, I did it. I said to myself something like, "Hmmm, what is the one most important thing I do or don't do that makes me unhappy?" And "What is the one most important thing I can do to step out of cycle of unhappiness and get happy again?"

I stood there under the trees simply feeling the questions in my body without trying to answer them in my mind. What happened next was extraordinary and unexpected.

A powerful, benign torrent of energy poured through my body. It was like being immersed in a bubbling spring of good feeling. The sensation was strong, like a rushing river, but it felt incredibly nurturing at the same time. A moment later I realized I could amplify the stream of good feeling if I moved my body and breathed deeply. I let my breath simply follow the sweet sensations that were pouring through me. In a matter of seconds, I was taking big, nurturing, easy breaths, lighting up places in me that had never felt so exhilaratingly alive.

I was so entranced by the new energy sensations streaming through me that I lost track of time. I don't know if it was fifteen minutes or fifty that I spent just walking among the trees, stretching and breathing, learning to navigate the new inner world I was opening up. As I did my breathing and stretching in the forest, another powerful awareness dawned in my body. It was so profound that I staggered and leaned up against a tree for support.

What I realized was that I had never really loved myself just as I was. I loved many people unconditionally—my daughter, other family members, several friends—but I had never given that same blessing to myself. At the core, I think I regarded myself as a failed self-improvement project. As I scanned back through my life, I saw how I'd always been at war with my own experience. If I felt sad, I tried to talk myself out of it and cheer myself up. If I had intense sexual feelings, I felt guilty about it. If I felt scared or lonely, I tuned those feelings out and opened the refrigerator.

Here was the one problem I'd been looking for! Our problem is that we learn to tune out our true sense of self in favor of a set of personas that deal with the world around us. Some of those personas are positive and useful: Mom's Helper, Dad's Buddy, Smart Kid, Problem-Solver. They help us be successful in the big world to come.

Other personas do not yield positive outcomes: Juvenile Delinquent, Sick Kid, Accident Waiting to Happen, Loner, Gossiper, Cheater. The reason those personas don't get positive results is because they're not designed to produce positive results. They're designed by our unconscious mind to reduce pain and keep us from losing entirely. For example, there was a bully in my third-grade class who would get up and kick everybody's marbles across the schoolyard if he lost. One time, he threw a basketball over the fence to keep his side from losing. The Bully is just one of the negative personas that come out under stress.

Whether it's a positive persona like Problem-Solver or a negative, pain-producing one such as Juvenile Delinquent, we often get so identified with our personas that we lose touch entirely with our own authentic feelings, needs, and desires. We split ourselves in two, with one part being who we really are and one part an amalgam of all the personas we developed to get along in whatever environment we find ourselves. We become like Mr. Duffy, the character in a James Joyce novel who "lived a short distance from his body."

If that was the one problem, what was the one solution? I could feel the truth of it in my body: Love yourself exactly as you are! Open your heart to yourself, no matter what you've done and been. Accept all of you into the wholeness of your expanded self. Embrace yourself, even the most painful of your personas and the most unforgiveable of your acts. Just love as much as you can from wherever you are. Each act of loving yourself expands your new sense of oneness with yourself, other people, and the world around you.

When I tell this story in public, there's often a brave soul who will stick up a hand and say, "Were you on drugs of some kind?" The answer is yes: I'd had a cup of decaf coffee. I happen to remember that because I had decided to kick real coffee when I moved to Colorado. During my grad-student years I'd developed a major coffee addiction; it was my way of keeping my brain working at the warp-speed that's necessary to earn/

survive a Ph.D. at Stanford. It worked, but by the time I got my degree I'd gone from one cup in the morning to drinking two cups at breakfast and four or five more throughout the day. I decided to use my move to Colorado as the beginning of my new caffeine-free life. Sad to say, my decaf phase only lasted until mid-semester before I returned with gusto to high-octane coffee.

As I stood under the trees I could feel the powerful flow of sensations begin to fade into the background. As the body sensations subsided, I became aware of a new sense of radiant clarity in my mind. It was as if the powerful rush of energy had cleansed my mind and left it with new insights that had practical applications. I could see how those insights were the basis of a new and expanded way of helping people.

The key insights that came from the experience:

- **Our problems stem from living, like Mr. Duffy "a short distance" from our bodies.** Due to early learning, we withdraw from pain and other unpleasant body feelings such as fear, anger, and sadness. This act of defensiveness divides us in half: the authentic, embodied self and the distant observer. The resulting split leads to discontent and even physical maladies. For example, the late John Sarno, M.D., the famous back-pain specialist at Rusk Rehabilitation Institute, discovered that only a tiny percentage of back pain needed surgery. He found that most back pain was caused by unconsciously tensing muscles from the low back up through the neck and shoulders. Specifically, these muscles tense up when you get angry and don't have any way to express it. It's the same set of muscles that make the hackles stand up on the back of a cat or dog. Dr. Sarno showed patients how to deal with their anger effectively and the back pain went away.

- **Love itself is a powerful healing force.** The act of loving the unlovable is the crucial action that restores us to wholeness. As I applied this principle, I found that under every one of my recurring problems was something I hadn't yet learned to love. For example, in my twenties I had a string of relationships with women that ended unhappily. Most of the time it was the woman who dumped me, making it easy for me to blame them and claim the victim position. After my experience in the Colorado woods, I began looking inward and found that the pattern was actually driven by my own fear of intimacy and pain from unacknowledged early childhood issues.

- **Once we've learned to feel and accept what's real in ourselves, we have the possibility of creating authentic relationships with others.** Up until then, we get locked into learned personas such as Shy Guy, Gossip Girl, Macho Man or Life of the Party. These personas keep us from connecting with others authentically. For example, my early life was dominated by my Fat Kid persona, and even after I lost the extra weight it took me years to accept and love the pain underneath that version of myself. Once I did, though, I finally was able to create lasting love with Katie.

The Aftermath

I had the opportunity to test out the principles immediately after my experience in the woods. I got a phone call from a woman I'd met a couple of days earlier at a party for new faculty. It was held every year just before fall semester began, an opportunity for the existing faculty to welcome the new recruits. At the party I'd probably met two dozen other faculty members and their partners, so I hadn't gotten to know any of them in any depth. That was soon to change!

Fran asked if she could come over and talk to me about an issue she was struggling with. I was a little surprised, given that we'd only met briefly, but I told her to come right over. When Fran arrived, I noticed right away that her breathing was short and shallow, her face was flushed pink and her hands were clenching. I invited her to sit down and asked her to tell me the reason for her agitation. It was a doozy. Her husband, a bespectacled middle-aged professor I'd also met at the party, had just told her he was having an affair with a graduate student.

Her words tumbled out. "One minute I'm a soccer-mom with two kids in middle school, married for twenty years to my college boyfriend. Then, Charlie says, 'Honey, I need to talk to you about something.' The next minute I'm a cheated-on wife in the middle of a scandal." (It's generally frowned upon for professors to sleep with their students. Graduate students are a grey area, though, because they can often be as old or older than their professors. The husband's paramour was a married woman in her 40s, but even so, I learned later that their relationship had become a subject of whispered conversations in the faculty lounge.

Based on the experience I'd just had in the woods, I worked with Fran in a completely different way than I might have the day before. Instead of trying to reassure her or calm her down, I went in the opposite direction. I invited her to come in from "a short distance" away from her body and let herself feel her emotions in all their intensity. What happened next changed her life, and mine.

I said, "Let go of trying to control your fear. Just put your attention on the sensations of the fear and be with it. Welcome the fear and love it as it is."

She closed her eyes and settled into her chair. Suddenly her breathing started to get faster and deeper. Soon she escalated into big, shuddering breaths, as if she had one foot on the accelerator and one foot on the brakes. I called that to her attention and invited her to take the brakes off and let her breathing do whatever it wanted to do. In a flash, she was taking the biggest breaths I'd ever seen in another person. What amazed me even more was that she no longer looked scared. Her facial expression was wide-eyed wonder, like a surfer in the sweet spot of the wave.

The intense deep breathing lasted another minute or two, then began to subside. Neither one of us said a word while she slowly came back down. When her breathing slowed to normal, she sat for another couple of minutes without speaking, a look of radiant wonder on her face. She looked utterly transformed from the fear-gripped woman of fifteen minutes earlier. She sat up straight in her chair, her posture completely different from her timid cringe when she first sat down. I could scarcely believe my eyes, but down inside me I could also feel a deep sense of satisfaction. What happened to me in the woods and what happened in front of my eyes with Fran were not fluke events. They were part of a guiding principle that would take me far beyond the limits of traditional therapy.

At that time, most of psychology and psychiatry was dominated by the notion of pathology. For example, anxiety was regarded as a symptom, with the goal being to eliminate it. The pathological view was, of course, extremely useful in certain areas of healing. In my early years the great medical miracle was the polio vaccine; in my later years the corona-virus virus vaccine was the latest triumph of the pathological view. In this approach, a pathogen is identified, and a pharmaceutical is designed to eliminate it. When it works, it often does look like a miracle.

The pathological view dominated in the early development of psychotherapy. Most of the early psychotherapists were medical doctors, so it's easy to see why they might adopt that view. However, the more the field developed, the less the pathological model worked. We discovered, as any experienced healing professional eventually will, that most human problems don't fit the pathological model very well.

For example, before Fran called me, she had phoned a friend, a psychiatrist who was in Fran's women's group. The psychiatrist immediately offered to call in a prescription for Valium, at the time the most popular treatment for anxiety. I'm not knocking pharmaceuticals, because I've seen the miracles they can produce; I'm using the example to highlight the problem of treating anxiety as a pathogen to be eradicated. This is a dangerous fallacy for many reasons, but one stands out: emotions are natural responses of the body that must be listened to, not silenced through drugs. Our emotions have been perfected over millions of years as signal systems. To ignore, deny or tune those signal systems out is done at great peril. For example, tuning out the millions-year-old signal system of needing to visit the bathroom can have spectacularly negative consequences. The signals of fear, anger and sadness, if ignored, can invite equivalent chaos in our personal lives.

Anxiety is another word for fear, one of several emotions that have a great deal to do with how you feel from moment to moment. Anger and sadness also play a large role in our daily experience. Each of those emotions is designed by nature to deliver a specific message.

The message of fear is "You're experiencing some kind of threat."

Anger's message is "You're experiencing or seeing some kind of violation or act of unfairness."

Sadness is a message of "You're experiencing a loss of some kind." Note that I use the phrase "of some kind," because the emotion can be a response to something on the outside or something of our own mental manufacture. For example, I've treated people for snake phobia who have never actually seen a snake in real life. Their anxiety was just as real as another man I treated who tripped while out hunting and fell into a nest of baby rattlesnakes.

I've learned, through my own life as well as in working with clients, that the feeling of happiness comes from how you feel about your other feelings. If you pay attention to your fear, anger, and sadness—tune in to them and open your mind to the messages coming from them—you get to be happy. If you tune out those same feelings, whether through drugs or distractions such as too much TV, you don't. For example, if you answer a ringing telephone right away, you're likely to be much happier than if you let it continue to ring all day but cover it with more and more pillows.

Phase Three: Into The Genius Zone

In the early 1980s I made a fortuitous connection with a prominent business consultant, Kate Ludeman, author of the book, *The Worth Ethic*. Kate read one of my books and got in touch with me about working with some of her corporate clients.

I had worked with executives from large corporations for many years, but I mainly saw them for individual problems such as back pain, anger management, and anxiety. Kate's work was about increasing the health of whole organizations, and in that context, I began to work with executive teams at Dell Computer, KLA Instruments, Motorola, and many others. Years later Kate and I would summarize this work in our book, *The Corporate Mystic*.

It was also through this work that I first had the insights that led to my book, *The Big Leap*. The two big concepts of that book—the Upper Limit Problem and the Genius Zone—became the foundations of my work with citizens of the corporate world.

Sometimes people ask me how long it took to write The Big Leap. I say, "A year, but I'd been thinking about it for 30 years." Since the 80s, my team and I have worked on-site or in our offices with about 1200 executives from a wide range of enterprises. The Big Leap work found a ready audience in the business world, in my view for two main reasons.

First, the Upper Limits work provides a friendly way to see your faults and flaws. You get a quick picture of the ways you sabotage yourself and see how those self-defeating programs are connected to fears you picked up earlier in your life. *The Big Leap* also gives you a prescription for overcoming those limitations, a roadmap to realizing your true potential.

The second major concept in The Big Leap is the Genius Zone. It's my contention that each of us carries within us a treasure-trove of unrealized potential.

I call *it genius*. The key to tapping into your genius is to discover the things you most love to do and that make your maximum positive contribution to your world.

This concept resonates with successful people, because they sense that they are functioning in what I call the Zone of Excellence. In that zone, you are doing things you're very good at and bring you rewards in money, recognition, and other valuables. However, there is a cost of staying too long in your Zone of Excellence. If you persist in neglecting your genius, you expose yourself to burn-out and its insidious cousin, rust-out—the chronic accumulation of stress over a long period of time.

I remember a turning-point conversation with a physician in the early 80s, during his first therapy session. It is emblematic of similar conversations with business executives, lawyers, and other successful professionals. Here's a pared-down version of what he told me: "I'm turning 40 in a couple of weeks, and it's thrown me into a panic. I've been in practice for fifteen years now and from the outside I've been very successful. My wife and kids are happy, I'm making close to a million dollars a year, we live in our dream house, and yet I feel like if I keep going this way it's going to kill me."

On the surface it looked like a case of overwork and burn-out—the classic recipe for a midlife crisis—but as we delved into what had brought him to this moment, he said something I didn't expect. He told me that a nightmare had instigated the panic. It surprised me because he was a very matter-of-fact guy, not the sort who's likely to talk about his dreams. In the unsettling dream, he was in a mountain cabin writing poetry, when somehow, he started to slide down the mountain. He realized he was sliding down into an operating theater and he panicked because he wasn't in his scrubs. He awoke hyperventilating and thrashing in his bed, with his wife saying, "Honey, wake up. You're having a bad dream."

I asked him what he thought the image of writing poetry in a mountain cabin meant. He surprised me again by saying he wrote poetry when he was a teenager and had even won an award for young poets. A light went on in my head, a moment of clarity about the distinction between the Excellence Zone and the Genius Zone. Here was a person who had functioned too long in his Excellence Zone. In so doing, he'd neglected his Genius Zone. He was a surgeon who wanted to be a poet again.

I asked him how long it had been since he'd written a poem. He burst into tears before the question was out of my mouth. It turned out he hadn't written a poem in decades. One of my therapeutic principles is to solve the problem on the spot, if at all possible. In that spirit, I handed him a pen and a piece of paper and said, "Let's solve that problem right now. I'd like you to write a short poem."

He pushed back in his chair and said, "I don't know if I can do that now. I've been a surgeon too long."

I didn't let him off the hook. I said, "Then write a short poem about being a surgeon too long."

He went along with it and produced the following poem:

> My hand is steady
> But my head is not.
> A surgeon with a monkey mind.

To me that's pure genius. It's a summary of his life condition, spare and elegant as any *haiku* ever written.

This story had a happy ending. He became a surgeon who turned his work into poetry. He even got a modicum of fame when several of his poems about surgery were printed in a medical journal. Most importantly, though, he made a graceful leap into his Genius Zone and rekindled his zest for life.

I've had similar conversations with business executives, doctors, lawyers and entertainers. The people who come to me often feel there is something missing, a sense of not using their full capabilities. I gave a name to what they're missing out on. I called it the Genius Zone, and, in *The Big Leap*, I offered a map to getting there. I'm very grateful that concepts from The Big Leap such as the Upper Limits Problem, the Genius Zone, and Einstein Time, have now entered the public lexicon. In recent years, I've been delighted to hear them pop up on late-night talk shows, sit-coms, and other popular media.

Summing Up

When I was in my early 30s I sat down one day and spent an hour getting clear on the big goals for my life. I came up with five goals, documented in my book, *Five Wishes*.

My first goal was to create a loving, long-lasting relationship with a woman. After creating a number of unfulfilling relationships in my teens and 20s, I was just beginning a new relationship with Katie. I really wanted it to work, but I didn't know yet where it would go.

My second goal was to live in a state of completion, in which I didn't have any significant unexpressed communications with the people in my life. As my stories show, I grew up in a complicated Southern family where secrets and long-withheld communication were constant features. Trying to unravel these things occupied my mind as a kid, and probably gave me as useful a training in family therapy as I got in graduate school. Based on all that, I wanted to create a life of serenity, free from the dramas caused by lies and secrets.

My third goal for my life was to learn to write clearly and from my heart about the things I found most useful in helping people change their lives. I had been trained in the academic style of writing, which requires authors to keep a distance from their subject. Particularly, you need to make sure your personal feelings stay out of the way. I wanted to go to the opposite extreme in my writing. For example, I was at the time writing a book about emotions. Rather than keeping an academic distance from my subject, I was examining my own feelings of sadness, anger, fear and joy. That book evolved into *Learning to Love Yourself*, which came out in 1982 and has remained steadily in print for forty years. The book's early success was greatly assisted by an awful review in a popular magazine, *Psychology Today*.

When the book came out, it began selling a modest couple of thousand books a month. Then, after about six months, a weird miracle happened. A book reviewer, R.D. Rosen, wrote a savage criticism of the emerging new genre called *Self Help*. He singled out *Learning to Love Yourself*; specifically, he took me to task for dropping academic distance and writing about my own feelings. He was outraged that a "formerly respectable" psychologist was daring to reveal his own inner world.

I felt hurt by the review but one day the phone rang with a cure for my blues. It was my publisher calling from New York, a high pitch of excitement in her voice: "Whatever you're doing out there, keep doing it. Suddenly we're selling ten thousand copies a month!" She hadn't heard about the review, and when I described it to her, we had a good laugh at the sweet irony of it all. Apparently, the reading public liked the very things that had so inflamed the reviewer.

My fourth and fifth goals were more diffuse: to learn as much as possible about the Creator Force in the universe and to savor all the moments of my life. Both of those goals are harder to quantify than the first three, but all in all, I'm happy with what I've discovered in the spiritual realm and how I've learned to appreciate the moments of my life, large and small. In my life now, I enjoy loading the dishwasher just as much as I enjoy being on stage at a conference.

I feel blessed that all my dreams have come true. Some of my goals, such as savoring my life or learning about the Creator Force, don't have an end-point; I hope to be soaking up more knowledge about the spiritual nature of the universe as I breathe my final breath.

Speaking of which, as I write this, I just turned 77. I'm in excellent health, thanks to good food, long walks, three hours of resistance training a week, a great marriage, fifty years of daily meditation, and some darn good luck. My granddad lived to 93, so I've got some good genes working for me. Whatever the future has in store for me, I'm just going to keep doing what I'm doing. When the time comes for my exit, I hope to be writing a final book, perhaps called *Having a Good Time Dying*.

AFTERWORD

I got an unexpected prophesy at a party forty years ago, a prediction about my elder years that seems to be coming true. A famous astrologer, the late Ed Steinbrecher, was a guest at the party. I'm an astrological ignoramus, so I took advantage of the opportunity to pepper Ed with questions about astrology and my sign, Aquarius. He asked for my birthdate and did a few quick calculations. "Lucky you," he said.

I asked him why.

"Because you're going to have a late-life surge of creativity and success." He went on to explain that I would always be creative but that it would come to full flower in the last part of my life.

Whether it was written in the stars or not, the prophesy has certainly come true. I've had the most amazing outpouring of creativity in the decade-plus since I turned sixty-five—nine published mystery novels (and five more in the pipeline), three non-fiction books, a screenplay, and the Big Leap Podcast. One of my high intentions for life was to create a job I'd never want to retire from, and it's come true far beyond my dreams.

I'm grateful for every minute of my life today. Thank you to all who have passed through my life in person or through books and media. I'm grateful for the space you've provided me to fulfill my creative potential. May you own that space for yourself and soar into the infinite realms of your own special genius.

www.ingramcontent.com/pod-product-compliance
Lightning Source LLC
Chambersburg PA
CBHW052005090426
42741CB00008B/1561